RESEARCH METHODS IN SPECIAL EDUCATION

D1489909

Applied Social Research Methods Series
Volume 37

APPLIED SOCIAL RESEARCH METHODS SERIES

RESEARCH METHODS IN SPECIAL EDUCATION

Donna M. Mertens
John A. McLaughlin

Applied Social Research Methods Series
Volume 37

SAGE Publications
International Educational and Professional Publisher
Thousand Oaks   London   New Delhi

For information address:

SAGE Publications, Inc.
2455 Teller Road
Thousand Oaks, California 91320

SAGE Publications Ltd.
6 Bonhill Street
London EC2A 4PU
United Kingdom

SAGE Publications India Pvt. Ltd.
M-32 Market
Greater Kailash I
New Delhi 110 048 India

Printed in the United States of America

Library of Congress Cataloging-in-Publication Data

Mertens, Donna M.
    Research methods in special education / Donna M. Mertens, John A.
McLaughlin
        p.   cm. — (Applied social research methods series; v. 37)
    Includes bibliographical references.
    ISBN 0-8039-4808-5. — ISBN 0-8039-4809-3 (pbk.)
        1. Special education—Research—United States—Methodology.
    2. Disabled—Education—Research—United States—Methodology.
    I. McLaughlin, John A. (John Adams), 1943–   .   II. Title.
    III. Series.
    LC3981.M47   1995
    371.9'072—dc20   94-22984

                99   10   9   8   7   6   5   4   3   2

Sage Project Editor: Susan McElroy

Contents

1

Introduction

- Mentally retarded children are hostile and dangerous individuals whose condition is hereditary, and who should be segregated from the rest of society.
- If you let deaf children use sign language, they will not be motivated to learn to speak and lip read, and they will not perform as well in school.

The above statements are examples of unsupported myths that have sadly affected the lives of children with disabilities (Gallagher, 1979; Van Cleve & Crouch, 1989). In the 1960s, for example, research was conducted that suggested that deaf children of deaf parents had higher scores than deaf children of hearing parents on reading, arithmetic, social adjustment, and writing, and were no different in terms of use of speech and lip reading (Meadow, 1967). Within a short time after the appearance of that research, a revolution occurred in deaf education such that between 1968 and 1978, the majority of deaf programs changed from oral communication to total communication (Moores, 1987).

Research can make contributions toward fundamental changes in educational practice. This is not to say that research by itself will be responsible for changes in practice, such as the dramatic changes in deaf education. Societal change is dependent in part on the use that is made of such information by politically oriented advocacy groups, such as the National Association of the Deaf. Nor does it suggest that the issue is closed regarding the most effective communication system for deaf people. Debate rages on as to which sign communication system is best, and this continues to be the type of empirical issue on which research can shed light.

In This Chapter

- The purposes and intended audiences for this book are introduced, along with reasons that research is important in special education.
- Trends and issues in special education are explored in terms of their implications for research methodology and the need for additional research.
- A discussion of philosophical orientations in research provides an organizing framework for the depiction of the steps typically followed in conducting research.

PURPOSE OF THIS BOOK

Teachers and other educational personnel find themselves face-to-face with children who need an appropriate education for which an adequate research base is lacking. Thus, not only is there a need for more research in special education, but there is also a need for more critical analysis of existing research and improvement of the quality of research in special education. Those who conduct research in special education must be aware of the implications of the unique context and special populations for their work. No research methods are unique to special education (Gaylord-Ross, 1990-1992; Switzky & Heal, 1990). Special education adopted its research methods from such other disciplines as psychology, ethnography, and anthropology.

This book explores ways to adapt those research methods to the special education context by providing the reader with a framework for critically analyzing and conducting research focusing on the specific special education context. Unique contextual factors and populations in special education have implications for research conceptualization, design, implementation, interpretation, and reporting. For example, the definition of who constitutes the special education population is not clear cut. Who should be labeled "at risk," disabled, or developmentally delayed? What are the implications of conducting or critiquing research that addresses different types of functional impairments (e.g., mental retardation vs. paralysis, or blindness vs. epilepsy)? These are the types of contextual issues specific to special education research that are addressed in this book.

The audience for this book includes those persons who intend to conduct or critically analyze research done with special education populations. The populations that are included are primarily those that are eligible for funds under the federal government's classification system of special education students in the Individuals with Disabilities Education Act (IDEA) of 1990; that is, mental retardation, hearing impairments, speech or language impairments, visual impairments, serious emotional disturbance, orthopedic impairments, other health impairments, specific learning disabilities, multiple disabilities, deafness/blindness, autism, and traumatic brain injury. (Readers interested in research with gifted students are referred to Buchanan & Feldhusen, 1991.) Additionally, the text includes discussion of infants and toddlers with disabilities, and persons with developmental delays and those at risk.

This text does not purport to replace research methodology texts (see, e.g., Ary, Jacobs, & Razavieh, 1990; Bogdan & Biklen, 1992; Borg & Gall, 1989; Harding, 1987; Kerlinger, 1973; Krathwohl, 1993; Lincoln & Guba, 1985; Marshall & Rossman, 1989; Nielsen, 1990) or educational assessment texts (see, e.g., Miller, 1991). Rather it explores the adaptation of research methods to the special education context by providing the researcher with a framework for critically analyzing and conducting research within the special education context. The reader who is unfamiliar with basic research methodology should plan to use this book in conjunction with another more comprehensive research methods text, such as those referenced in this paragraph.

TRENDS AND ISSUES AFFECTING SPECIAL EDUCATION RESEARCH

Special education research is affected by political, social, and contextual factors that are unique to its functioning. These factors have implications for methodology at every stage of the research process.

Political and Legislative Changes

Many issues stem from external forces that define the milieu in which special educators operate. The Education of the Handicapped Act, passed in 1975, was changed to the Individuals with Disabilities Education Act (IDEA) in 1990. IDEA (and its predecessor legislation) resulted in fewer students with disabilities being educated in separate schools or classrooms. The effect of this change has at least two methodological implications. First, identification of research subjects became more complicated, and second, placement in many schools resulted in an increase in the variability of contextual factors (Wang, Reynolds, & Walberg, 1990). The identification of the independent variable in studying the effects of mainstreaming becomes a more complex issue, which is not satisfactorily resolved in most special education research (Gallagher, 1990; Wang et al., 1990).

Reform Movement

Although challenges from IDEA continue to confront special education researchers, new challenges emerged as calls for reform in education resounded throughout the country in the decade of the 1980s. In a summary of literature related to special education and the reform movement, The National Center on Educational Outcomes (1991) recognized the turmoil in education and the resulting cries for accountability as part of a massive reform movement. However, the school reform literature has not addressed the role of special education in the reform movement. Ferguson (1989) noted that there has been "... almost unanimous silence about the extent to which the analysis and recommendations apply to, or affect students with handicaps in public special education" (p. 26).

Total Inclusion Movement

Despite the silence in the commission reports (e.g., National Commission on Excellence in Education, 1983), special educators have not been silent about their need to be included in the reform movement (National Center on Educational Outcomes, 1991). Special education is embroiled in a time of change and reform that is an outgrowth of more than a decade of struggling with the implications of the original mainstreaming legislation. A strong voice from within the special education community is calling for total inclusion of students with disabilities, in the form of a merger of general and special education (Biklen, Ferguson, & Ford, 1989; Lipsky & Gartner, 1989), and general education is taking up this call as well (National Association of State Boards of Education, 1992).

NEED FOR ADDITIONAL RESEARCH

With the passage of IDEA, the reform movement, and the call for total inclusion, special education is on the threshold of significant changes in practice without the research base that is necessary to make the critical choices for the children in the greatest need. Gallagher (1990) stated, "It is not enough to point out the shortcomings of the existing system . . . we need more evidence of the virtues of the new movement" (p. 36).

Wang et al. (1990) recognized the role that research can play in the complex challenges that face special educators. They stated:

> The field of special education seems particularly open to theories and practices, even before they are thoroughly tested. There are millions of children whose problems have been diagnosed in terms of cognitive rigidity . . . lack of sensory integration, perceptual problems, auditory sequencing difficulties, or unusual WISC profiles—all of which add up to zero or near zero validity when later tested for instructional relevance. The solution to these problems is a particular responsibility of the researchers in the special education community who should call for decent levels of evidence before practices are allowed to enter the field in broad ways. (p. 202)

PHILOSOPHICAL ORIENTATION OF THE BOOK

Educational researchers are engaged in a paradigm struggle in defining approaches to research. A paradigm is a worldview that includes certain philosophical assumptions about the nature of knowledge (i.e., epistemology). The dominant orientation in educational research historically has been derived from the philosophical orientation of positivism. Epistemologically, positivism is represented by the rationalistic paradigm, which typically employs a quantitative research design (Guba & Lincoln, 1989; Nielsen, 1990). Alternative perspectives have emerged (e.g., the constructivist paradigm) that have typically been associated with qualitative research designs and are described as contextual, inclusive, experiential, involved, socially relevant, multimethodological, and inclusive of emotions and events as experienced. It is beyond the scope of the present text to explore the underlying axioms of each paradigm (see Guba & Lincoln, 1989; Nielsen, 1990); however, researchers should be familiar with the paradigm debate, read and reflect on this topic, and establish their own worldview as it affects their research activities.

In terms of philosophical orientation, researchers must not only identify their epistemological worldview, but also their ideological perspectives; that is, the researcher's position as to the use of research for political purposes. Langenbach, Vaughn, and Aagaard (1994) identified two ideological views prevalent in the research community as *status quo* and *reform*. Researchers who are not overtly political in their interpretation of their data are oriented toward the status quo. Researchers who explore political explanations of their data move into the realm of reform. These two positions, status quo and reform, actually represent two end points on a continuum, with many researchers falling in the middle. This overlay of ideology can be used within either the positivist or the constructivist orientation to research.

Feminist researchers serve as one example of scholars who have written extensively about the reform ideology in research, and their perspectives have particular importance for researchers in special education for two reasons. First, "women with disabilities traditionally have been ignored not only by those concerned about disability but also by those examining women's experiences" (Asch & Fine, 1992, p. 141). Almost all research on disabled men and women seems to simply assume the irrelevance of gender, race, ethnicity, sexual orientation, or class. Second, Fine and Asch (1988) made the point that people with disabilities comprise a minority group, and most of their problems can and must be understood in a minority group framework. As a minority group, persons with disabilities have differential power and receive differential and pejorative treatment. As the authors of this text, we are sensitive to issues related to bias based on ethnicity, gender, class, and disability, and we include implications of the reform ideology in our exploration of working with special education populations throughout the research process.

THE RESEARCH PROCESS AND THE ORGANIZATION OF THIS BOOK

The typical process of planning and conducting a research study was used as the basis for organizing the information in this book (see Figure 1.1). We recognize that the research process is never as linear as it is portrayed in Figure 1.1, and that (especially with qualitative designs) the process can be very iterative in nature. However, our goal is to depict the typical steps in conducting research, even though a researcher may be doing footwork that more resembles the cha-cha than a straightforward stroll.

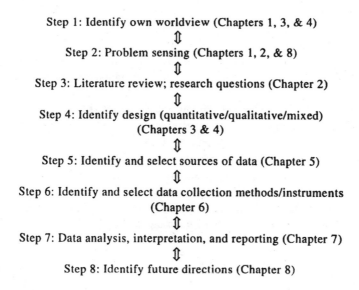

Step 1: Identify own worldview (Chapters 1, 3, & 4)
⇕
Step 2: Problem sensing (Chapters 1, 2, & 8)
⇕
Step 3: Literature review; research questions (Chapter 2)
⇕
Step 4: Identify design (quantitative/qualitative/mixed)
(Chapters 3 & 4)
⇕
Step 5: Identify and select sources of data (Chapter 5)
⇕
Step 6: Identify and select data collection methods/instruments
(Chapter 6)
⇕
Step 7: Data analysis, interpretation, and reporting (Chapter 7)
⇕
Step 8: Identify future directions (Chapter 8)

Figure 1.1. Steps in the Research Process

Research in special education is used to explore the use of the literature review to define the theoretical framework and to identify research questions, variables, and the most appropriate approach to the research (Chapter 2). Specific implications of quantitative and qualitative research designs are critically evaluated in special education research (Chapters 3 and 4). Issues such as the identification of subjects, the definition of populations, the heterogeneity of subjects, appropriate sampling techniques, ethics (Chapter 5), and reliability, validity, and accommodations for populations with disabilities are examined for data collection (Chapter 6). Data analysis and interpretation issues are discussed in terms of appropriate use of analytic methods and the impact of analytic technique and results on conclusions (Chapter 7). Future directions are explored in terms of methodological and substantive issues (Chapter 8).

The reader who is interested in actually planning a research study can use the organizational framework in this text in conjunction with Hedrick, Bickman, and Rog's (1993) book on planning a research study, which provides many examples of practical procedures for planning applied research.

QUESTIONS FOR
DISCUSSION AND APPLICATION

1. What myths in education do you know about that influenced educators to behave in ineffective ways (e.g., physical punishment is a good way to discipline)?

2. How has research been helpful to you in your work?

3. What is your opinion as to the usefulness of research to the parent, teacher, counselor, or administrator in special education?

4. What issues can you identify that are in need of additional research?

5. What trends are occurring in special education that can influence research methodology and topics?

6. What trends are occurring outside of special education that can influence special education research methodology and topics?

2

Literature Review

It is difficult to think of a researcher undertaking a research project without some specific purpose in mind. One of the primary purposes of research is to generate information that will increase understanding and identify successful practices or products. The researcher does not start from ground zero; there is a prior knowledge base established by other researchers. It is doubtful that there is any topic in special education that has not been addressed in some research endeavor. The professional literature serves as a major resource to researchers as they plan, implement, interpret, and report their research. The objective of this chapter is to orient the reader to the strategies associated with the conduct and use of the literature review. The information in this chapter serves as a bridge to subsequent chapters, which describe other steps in the research process.

In This Chapter

- The purposes of conducting the literature review, and sample research questions and hypotheses, are presented.
- Sources from which the literature can be drawn are identified.
- Search procedures for identifying and selecting appropriate literature are explained.
- Various procedures the researcher can employ to aggregate the literature selected for review are discussed.
- Questions for critically analyzing literature reviews in research are provided.

PURPOSES OF THE LITERATURE REVIEW

Remember your last vacation? If you are like most people, you probably spent substantial time planning your trip. You considered what you wanted to accomplish, your destination, what you would do during your vacation, and the items you needed to do these things. While for some people research is not a vacation, it does require planning if it is going to generate the required information. Just like vacation planning, personal experience is a valuable resource in planning research, but even the vacation planner goes beyond experience to consult travel brochures and maps. A major resource for the researcher at the planning stage of research is the professional literature.

Summarize Extant Research. The researcher may approach the literature with a number of purposes in mind. First, the intent may be to summarize the extant research to inform the reader of what is known about the subject, that is, what research has already been conducted. A by-product may be a publication that could become a resource to practitioners. That is, the review may identify how the results of research might be applied in the delivery of services to persons with disabilities. For example, O'Donnell and Livingston (1991) conducted a review of research on the relationship between low vision and the cognitive, motor, and social development of young children. The authors cited research that supported various approaches and optical aids that might be used by practitioners to enhance development in these areas.

Gaps in Knowledge Base. A second important purpose of the literature review is the identification of weaknesses or gaps in the current knowledge base. For example, O'Donnell and Livingston found that previous researchers had not studied the effects of using low vision optical devices on the cognitive development of infants with low vision.

Thus, the literature review informs the researcher of the results of previously conducted studies. The review may be used to inform practitioners of successful practices, and it may also enable the researcher to identify the next logical step in the research chain. This need for further research may go beyond omissions by previous researchers to new ways of addressing the research problem, different measurement, and analysis techniques.

Interpretation of Findings. While the literature review is a major resource to researchers who are playing out their role as planners, there is a third purpose of the literature review. Just like being on a vacation, things do not always go as planned in research. It is often necessary to return to the literature throughout the research to obtain information to help explain expected and unexpected findings. For example, Cole, Mills, Dale, and Jenkins (1991) investigated the effects of integrating preschool children with disabilities with those of the same age developing normally. In their discussion of the study findings, the authors proposed multiple explanations for observed interactions between intervention strategies and subject classification. To support these propositions, they cited several previous studies.

In another study, Fox (1989) explained the discrepancies between her findings and similar studies by comparing the differences in populations studied. Her students had learning disabilities, while other studies included subjects who were identified as being mentally retarded. In the same article, Fox cited similar studies in which the same results were observed, and used this consistency across studies to support her conclusions and implications for practice.

The researcher can be thought of as a problem solver. Because the goal of the research is to increase understanding, the problem is a gap in the knowledge base. To solve the problem, the researcher must establish an empirical information base from which to draw conclusions and make recommendations about the problem.

Conceptual Framework. The literature helps the researcher construct a theoretical or conceptual framework. The framework becomes the standard for the proposed research, a statement of what the researcher expects to observe as the research project unfolds. It communicates expected outcomes, activities or interventions necessary to achieve these outcomes, and resources that must be available to support the intervention. The conceptual framework tells the researcher what information to collect, what should be measured to increase understanding about the problem addressed in the study.

One example of a conceptual framework is that developed by The National Longitudinal Transition Study of Special Education Students (NLTS) to explain the transition experiences and outcomes for youth with disabilities (DeStefano & Wagner, 1991). The NLTS was designed to serve as a framework for understanding and predicting the relationship between school-based special education experiences and postschool outcomes. Researchers interested in studying relationships in this domain could use the NLTS framework as a guide for designing and interpreting their research. Another conceptual framework was developed by the National Center on Educational Outcomes at the College of Education, the University of Minnesota, to explain educational outcomes for children and youth with disabilities (Ysseldyke, Thurlow, Bruininks, Gilman, Deno, McGrew, & Shriner, 1993). This group was established to provide leadership in the development of educational outcomes for all students with disabilities.

RESEARCH QUESTIONS AND HYPOTHESES

The literature review serves as a foundation for forming research questions. Hedrick, Bickman, and Rog (1993) suggest that the research questions operationalize the objectives of the proposed research. They focus the research hypotheses and clarify what information needs to be collected from what sources under what conditions. Simply stated, a hypothesis is an if . . . then statement. For example, a hypothesis could state that if subjects are exposed to a particular intervention, then they will behave in a certain predictable manner. Kerlinger (1973) states that: "the hypothesis is a conjectural statement, a tentative proposition, about the relationship between two or more phenomena or variables" (p. 12).

Framing the research question can be a difficult task for beginning researchers. Hedrick et al. (1993) present a taxonomy for categorizing research questions that includes four categories of questions: descriptive, normative, correlative, and impact. Each is briefly discussed within the context of research in special education.

Descriptive research questions are designed to produce information about what is happening in relation to the target of the research. For example, the researcher might want to describe certain characteristics of the participants in an intervention, or the prevalence of a particular disability within a specific domain. Such a research question might ask: What is the prevalence of mental retardation in black middle school children?

Normative research questions go beyond description, requiring that the information generated in response to the descriptive research question be compared to some standard or expected observation. Because special education has minimum requirements regarding most aspects of the service delivery system, a normative research question might ask: Were individual education plans (IEPs) in place before the placement was made, as is required by the minimum service delivery requirements?

We noted that a great deal of research is conducted to identify relationships to enable the explanation of phenomena. One avenue for examining relationships is the *correlative* research question. As Hedrick et al. point out, data derived in response to such questions indicate the strength and direction of a relationship between two or more variables, not causality. For example, the special education researcher might ask: What is the relationship between the size of family and the presence of emotional disturbance in siblings? If a strong positive relationship were found, this would not lead to the conclusion that large families cause emotional disturbance in siblings. Such a relational finding would suggest the need for further study to uncover the causal relationships.

Impact research questions are the last category offered in the Hedrick et al. taxonomy. Here the researcher's aim is to identify effects, to establish causal links between an independent variable (the intervention) and a dependent variable (the anticipated change). According to the Hedrick et al. framework, there are two types of effects that the researcher might investigate: *simple* and *relative*. In the Stinson, Gast, Wolery, and Collins (1991) study of the impact of an intervention (praise) on a behavior (learning a definition), they asked a simple impact question: Do students with moderate retardation who are praised immediately after correct sight reading learn more word definitions than students who receive delayed praise? If the researchers chose (and this is good practice) to explore the impact of the intervention on other related outcomes (e.g., self-esteem), additional questions could address relative effects. A sample hypothesis for an impact study might state: If students with moderate retardation are presented with a praise statement after correct sight-word reading, then they will learn more definitions than students who receive delayed praise.

In sum, the literature review serves many purposes. It establishes a historical perspective on the intended research and provides a vision of the need for additional research. But how does the researcher identify the salient literature to include in the review? There are several tools available to researchers to assist them in their review of the literature.

RESOURCES TO SUPPORT
THE LITERATURE REVIEW

Locating sources for the literature review is the first challenge for the prospective author. Critically analyzing the research articles and reports and aggregating the information into a usable form are the next challenges. The purpose of this section is to provide insights into the location of the literature. We should note, however, that while the literature is a primary information support, it is historical by nature. Therefore, researchers are well advised to consult other researchers and practitioners in the field of interest. According to Hedrick et al. (1993), such discussions may reveal current trends and issues, or new information which has yet to be found in the literature. Attending professional conferences, such as the annual meeting of the American Educational

Research Association or the Council for Exceptional Children, where research is reported provides an excellent opportunity for such dialogue. It should be noted that each disability area is represented by a professional organization, and these would also be good sources of information.

Secondary Sources

Often a literature review begins with reading secondary sources, that is, a synthesis of research findings on a particular topic. Any publication that is written by an author who did not conduct the research is considered a secondary source. Literature reviews are considered secondary sources, as are textbooks and reference books. An excellent example of a secondary source that could be used by the researcher in the planning phase of the research is Scruggs and Mastropieri (1992), which contains several papers on research and methodology related to learning and behavioral disabilities. Other secondary source handbooks of import in special education include the works of Wang, Reynolds, and Walberg (1987-1989), and Gaylord-Ross (1990-1992).

Primary Sources

Primary sources include publications that are prepared by the researcher who conducted the research. Because this type of report is considered to be more reliable, the review of literature should depend to a large extent on citations from primary sources. More than likely, the references will come from research journals, dissertations, or the final reports of research projects. There are a number of journals presenting research that could serve as a resource to researchers who are contemplating investigations of topics associated with persons with disabilities. Several journals that might serve as a resource to the researcher are listed in Table 2.1. Other important sources include final reports from research projects supported through public and private funding agencies, as well as reports to Congress by federal agencies. For example, the U.S. Office of Special Education Programs submits an Annual Report to Congress on the status of service delivery programs for students with disabilities (U.S. Department of Education, 1993a), and publishes a data dictionary that includes definitions of key terms in special education legislation (U.S. Department of Education, 1993b).

Table 2.1

Selected Journals Containing Special Education Resource Information

---

American Annals of the Deaf
American Journal on Mental Retardation
Annals of Dyslexia
Australia and New Zealand Journal of Developmental Disabilities
Behavioral Disorders
British Journal of Special Education
Canadian Journal of Special Education
Career Development for Exceptional Individuals
Education and Training in Mental Retardation
Exceptional Children
Exceptionality: A Research Journal
International Journal of Disability, Development and Education
Journal of Autism and Developmental Disorders
Journal of Early Intervention
Journal of Learning Disabilities
Journal of Special Education
Journal of Speech and Hearing Research
Journal of the Association for Persons With Severe Handicaps
Learning Disability Quarterly
Mental Retardation
Research in Developmental Disabilities
Volta Review

Databases

Conducting a review of literature can be exhausting; however, the development of computerized databases has eased the process. Marcaccio (1992) has prepared an extensive description of on-line computer literature/bibliographic information bases. And Cooper and Hedges (1994) provide a comprehensive review of literature search sources that furnish access to journals, books, unpublished technical reports, conference papers, and government publications. An excellent resource guide and process is also offered for identifying fugitive literature.

An essential first step in the process is generating a list of key words that will guide the search through the various written and electronic references. These key words are topic- or subject-oriented and are used to navigate indexes to the resources to identify relevant articles, reports, texts, and so on. Identifying key words is an emergent process. The researcher may start by generating the key words based on experience and previous readings. After some useful references have been located, the researcher may modify the list by dropping those that did not yield appropriate citations, and adding new words suggested by other authors. The development of the key word lists is made easier by consulting various thesauri linked to reference indexes, such as the *Thesaurus of ERIC Descriptors* (1990) and the *Thesaurus of Psychological Index Terms* (1988).

Fuchs and Fuchs (1986) employed an effective multistep search process. First, they used the *Thesaurus of Psychological Index Terms* to identify key words or topics. Next, they searched three on-line computerized information bases: (1) Educational Resources Information Center (ERIC), with abstracts from Research in Education and the Current Index to Journals in Education; (2) Comprehensive Dissertation Abstracts; and (3) Psychological Abstracts. Third, the authors selected journals that had a high probability of having research related to their topic. Using the same key words, they conducted a manual search of the journals for a 10-year period. Finally, they distinguished salient research from the articles identified through the above steps for review. Mastropieri, Scruggs, and Shiah (1991) conducted an integrated review of research related to mathematics instruction for students with learning disabilities. These authors followed a similar approach to that of Fuchs and Fuchs. However, they also conducted a manual search of the Exceptional Child Education database, using a key word process.

AGGREGATING INFORMATION
FOR A LITERATURE REVIEW

Once located, the literature must be critically reviewed. The criteria presented at the end of each chapter in this book can be used to critically review special education research. Cooper (1989) provided another framework for critical anaylsis of research, as well as a variety of methods for aggregating the results of studies in a literature review. The purpose of this section is to provide insights into the analysis and synthesis of literature from two perspectives: the integrated literature review and meta-analysis.

The *integrated literature review* is a process that requires the researcher to capture all the relevant literature, especially primary sources, critically analyze it, and produce a written representation of the current knowledge about a certain topic and conclusions that can be drawn from that knowledge base. Typically, the researcher looks at the evidence that supports various conclusions, areas needing further research, as well as research paths that have proven to be blind alleys. Further, the reviewer investigates the common and unique research approaches, exploring ways in which they were productive or unproductive. Cooper's (1989) guidelines can be used to determine potential threats to the validity of conclusions drawn from integrated reviews, and for making decisions about the inclusion of articles in the review.

Storey and Horner's (1991) study of social validation research methods provides one example of an integrated review in special education. Social validation research examines the value of having persons with disabilities evaluate research conducted on issues of central import to them—the services they receive, the policies and organizational structures that drive service delivery, as well as their own behaviors, skills, and values. Persons with disabilities were asked to judge the social value and significance of the research. Storey and Horner reviewed the current practice of social validation research. Their review addressed the social validation methods, methodological issues, and conclusions. As a result of their integrated review, they were able to confirm the importance of social validation and provide insightful suggestions to researchers and practitioners who would use the method.

Where the integrated research is based on a conceptual synthesis of research findings, the *meta-analysis approach* uses additional analyses to aggregate the findings of studies and reach conclusions (Glass, McGraw, & Smith, 1981). Meta-analysis is a quantitative synthesis of the existing research. Using primary source information from the literature, the meta-analyst establishes empirical evidence to increase understanding about a particular theory.

In meta-analysis, the researcher is addressing studies that have attempted to establish a causal relationship between some intervention and an outcome. Typically, an effect size is established for each study in the sample of studies drawn for the meta-analysis. The effect size is then compared across studies the analyst has identified in the literature. Effect size is discussed at greater length in Chapter 6 as a data analysis strategy.

Fuchs and Fuchs (1986) conducted a meta-analysis of studies centering on the effects of formative evaluation on student achievement. Based on analysis of 21 separate studies, the authors concluded that formative evaluation techniques positively influence student achievement. Kavale (1984) presented a comprehensive review of the advantages to using meta-analysis techniques to synthesize the literature in special education.

White, Taylor, and Moss (1992) reported a combined meta-analysis and integrative review that addressed the efficacy of parental involvement in early intervention programs. The authors first used trained coders to systematically describe and evaluate studies according to the intervention employed, target subject, information collection methods, and the study design. The studies were then subjected to a meta-analysis in which effect sizes were created and compared across studies.

There are both many driving and many restraining forces to using meta-analysis. While it does offer a systematic and objective method of aggregating the results of a large number of studies on a specific topic, this approach also suffers from the same threats that are faced in integrative research efforts, that is, the exhaustive nature of the retrieval process and the diversity of research quality in the studies selected. Guskin (1984) provides a useful discussion of the potential problems associated with employing meta-analyses in place of the integrated review procedures described by Cooper. The approach used by White et al. (1992) provides an excellent method for overcoming these threats.

QUESTIONS TO CRITICALLY ANALYZE
THE LITERATURE REVIEW

1. Is the review current, using research that is recent enough to have applicability to the proposed research?
2. Is the review based predominantly on primary research, rather than on secondary or opinion pieces?
3. Does the review establish a need for the study?
4. Does the review provide a critical analysis of existing literature, recognizing the strengths and weaknesses of current research?
5. Is the research review objective, free from the biases of the reviewer?
6. Does the review provide enough information to support the research theoretical framework and research questions posed?
7. Does the review provide sufficient information to guide the research procedures, including the identification of subjects, selection of data collection and analysis processes, as well as appropriate reporting strategies?

QUESTIONS AND ACTIVITIES FOR DISCUSSION AND APPLICATION

1. What are the purposes of the literature review?
2. How do the three different types of literature sources compare?
3. What are the essential steps in the review process?
4. What are the commonalities and differences between the integrated literature review and the meta-analysis?
5. How does the literature review relate to the other steps in the research process—selection of sample, identification of the research design, information collection and analysis strategies, the discussion of findings, as well as conclusions and recommendations?
6. Conduct an integrated literature review and apply the criteria for critical analysis found at the close of each chapter in this text (or those provided by Cooper, 1989).

3

Quantitative Research Methods

This chapter is designed for both the producer and the consumer of research. As a potential producer of research, your worldview, initial conceptualization of your research problem, and readings of related literature may have led you to conclude that a quantitative approach to research is most appropriate for you. As a consumer of research, you can use this chapter to identify the designs used in extant research studies and their corresponding strengths and weaknesses.

In This Chapter

- The concepts of internal and external validity are explored in terms of special education research.
- Seven types of quantitative research approaches are explained with special education examples: experimental, quasi-experimental, single group, causal comparative, correlational, single-subject designs, and survey research.
- Challenges associated with the use of quantitative designs in special education are discussed.
- Questions for critical analysis of each of the quantitative approaches are provided.

Quantitative research is rooted in the positivist paradigm, which holds that the purpose of research is to develop our confidence that a particular knowledge claim about educational phenomena is true or false by collecting evidence in the form of objective observations of relevant phenomena (Borg & Gall, 1989). Research design can be defined as a process of creating an empirical test to support or refute a knowledge claim.

EXPERIMENTAL, QUASI-EXPERIMENTAL, AND SINGLE-GROUP DESIGNS

A research design basically specifies who gets (or got) what treatment when. Researchers choose their designs based not only on their worldviews and research questions, but also on the logistics of their research settings. Three broad categories of research designs are discussed in this section: experimental, quasi-experimental, and single-group designs. We discuss one example of each type of design; the reader is referred to the general research methods texts referenced in Chapter 1 for more in-depth discussions of these design options. To depict the features of each design, a coding system is used with the following symbols:

R — Random assignment of subjects to conditions
X — Experimental treatment
O — Observation of the dependent variable (e.g., pretest, posttest, or interim measures)

The *independent variable* is the variable that is manipulated (e.g., teaching strategy). For example, a researcher could compare two teaching methods: new and traditional. The new method would be given to the *experimental group* and would be called the experimental treatment (X). The traditional method would be given to the *control group*. The *dependent variable* is the variable that is affected by (depends on) the independent variable (e.g., academic achievement).

Experimental Designs

True experimental designs use comparison groups and random assignment of subjects to conditions. One such design used in special education research is discussed here.

Single-Factor Multiple Treatment Designs. This design includes a control group and randomized assignment to three or four groups. Beirne-Smith (1991) used a three-group design to investigate the effect of peer tutoring on the computational skills of children with learning disabilities. Her independent variable was teaching method and her dependent variable was computational skill. She cited research which suggested that peer tutors were helpful for teaching reading skills, and that a "counting on" procedure was more effective than a rote memory approach to teaching simple computational skills. She combined this information to test the effect of peer tutoring using a counting on approach (X1), peer tutoring with a rote memory approach (X2), and a control group that received ongoing classroom instruction on math facts. Her design looked like this:

```
R   O   X1   O
R   O   X2   O
R   O        O
```

If experimenters are unable to randomly assign subjects to conditions, then they may choose a quasi-experimental approach.

Quasi-Experimental Designs

Quasi-experimental designs are those that are "almost true" experimental designs, except that the researcher studies the effect of the treatment on intact groups, rather than being able to randomly assign subjects to the experimental or control groups. One quasi-experimental design commonly used in special education research is briefly described here.

Non-Equivalent Control-Group Design. Wilson and Sindelar (1991) designed a quasi-experimental study in which they were unable to randomly assign their subjects because they had 62 subjects from nine schools, and subjects were assigned to instructional groups of 3 to 5 students, based on their school schedules. This example illustrates both a legitimate research design and also why experimental designs are difficult to implement in special education research because of barriers to randomization.

As with experimental designs, quasi-experimental designs can involve more than two groups, and their control group can receive an alternative treatment (as opposed to no treatment). Wilson and Sindelar were interested in the effect of using different teaching strategies on solving word problems with students with learning disabilities. The traditional approach to teaching math was called "sequencing," and involved teaching math facts first (i.e., computation of addition and subtraction problems), followed by word problems. The experimental approach was called "strategy" and involved a direct teaching strategy to solve word problems (X1). They had a third condition that combined sequencing and strategy (X2), thus, their design looked like this:

```
O   X1   O
-------------------------------
O   X2   O
-------------------------------
O        O
```

If it is not possible to use comparison groups, researchers may choose to use a single-group design.

Single-Group Designs

While this design does have many weaknesses, Borg and Gall (1989) state that it is justified under circumstances in which the researcher is attempting to change attitudes, behavior, or knowledge that are unlikely to change without the introduction of an experimental treatment. One pre-experimental single group design commonly used in special education research is briefly described here.

One-Group Pretest-Posttest Design. This design is often used to test effects of curriculum interventions. For example, Mertens and Rabiu (1992) used this design to test the effects of using cooperative learning strategies and computer-assisted instruction on deaf college students' learning of educational psychology principles and their attitudes toward computers. The researchers administered a pretest of students' knowledge and attitudes, implemented the treatment, and then used a posttest. This design is represented as follows:

O X O

Despite the weaknesses associated with this design, it may be necessary to use it in a situation in which it is not possible to have a control group because the school does not allow differential provision of services.

INTERNAL AND EXTERNAL VALIDITY

Within the positivist tradition, two tests of knowledge claims exist: (1) Is the knowledge claim true in *this* situation? (internal validity); (2) Is the knowledge claim true in *other* situations? (external validity or generalizability). In the next section we discuss the terms *internal validity* and *external validity*, ways to minimize threats to internal and external validity by using various research designs, and reasons why it can be difficult or impossible to apply these designs in special education research.

Internal Validity

Internal validity means that the changes that are observed in the dependent variable are due to the effect of the independent variable, and not some other unintended variables (known as *extraneous variables*). If extraneous variables are controlled, then the results are assumed to be due to the treatment and, therefore, the study is said to be internally valid. Extraneous variables that are not controlled become rival or competing explanations for the research results. Nine of the extraneous variables that can threaten internal validity are defined with examples (Campbell & Stanley, 1963; Cook & Campbell, 1979):

Threats to Internal Validity

History: events that happen during the course of the study that can influence the results.

Example: You are studying the effect of an integration program on people's attitudes toward individuals with disabilities. During your study, the mayor of the city declares it "Persons With Disabilities Capabilities Week," and the city is blanketed with a media campaign extolling the capabilities of persons with disabilities. This event could have an impact on people's attitudes, and it is not the treatment that you have in mind.

Maturation: biological or psychological changes in the subjects during the course of the study, such as becoming stronger, more coordinated, or tired as the study progresses.

Example: You may be interested in the development of social skills in children with severe disabilities who are integrated into their neighborhood schools. Generally, as children mature (i.e., grow older), their social skills improve. How would you know whether the change in their social skills was the effect of integration, or simply that the children had become more mature?

Testing: becoming "test-wise" by having taken a pretest that is similar to the posttest. Single-group designs are especially vulnerable to testing, history, and maturation because of a lack of a control group.

Example: The subjects know what to expect, learn something from the pretest, or become sensitized to what kind of information to tune in to during the study because of their experience with the pretest.

Instrumentation: another threat to validity in studies that use both pre- and posttests, or in observational studies in which the researcher serves as the data collection instrument. It arises when there is a change in the instrument during the course of the study.

Example: If a pretest and a posttest were used, it is possible that one test might be easier than the other. Thus, changes observed on the dependent variable would be due to the nature of the instrument and not the effect of the independent variable.

Statistical Regression: occurs when the researcher uses extreme groups as the subjects (i.e., students at the high or low end of the normal curve).

Example: If you select students who score at the 25th percentile on an achievement measure, and then test them again on a similar measure at the conclusion of the study, their scores could increase simply because of statistical regression, rather than because of your treatment. This is due to the role that chance and error play in test scores. We cannot measure achievement with 100% precision. Therefore, there is always an element of error in any measurement. If we have selected students from the bottom of the normal curve, then by chance it is most likely that their scores will go up (because they are already at the bottom, it is unlikely that they will go down). Statistical regression is a particular problem in special education research, especially when researchers try to use the original test data, by which the students were selected/identified for special education, as part of the study.

Differential Selection: If subjects with different characteristics are in the experimental and control groups, then differences in performance on the dependent variables may be due to group differences, and not necessarily due to the treatment or independent variable. Quasi-experimental designs are especially vulnerable to differential selection because of the lack of randomized assignment.

Example: In Kluwin and Moores's (1985) study, their independent variable was educational placement (comparing students in mainstreamed and self-contained classes for students who are deaf), and their dependent variable was math achievement. They found that the mainstreamed deaf students had higher math achievement. Could they conclude from this that mainstreaming results in higher math achievement? Not necessarily. It may be that those deaf students who are mainstreamed have higher initial cognitive abilities, and they would have had higher math achievement no matter where they were educated. When differential selection is a threat to validity, it is necessary to collect as much information as possible about the background characteristics of the groups, so that the experimental and control groups can be compared for important preexisting differences.

Experimental Mortality: the effect of subjects who drop out during the course of the study. It becomes a threat to validity if subjects differentially drop out of the experimental and control groups.

Example: Suppose you have a new strategy for teaching reading to learning disabled students during a special summer program. The experimental group gets the new strategy and the control group gets the traditional approach. During the study, many of the higher ability students drop out of the experimental group. At the end, the scores for the lower ability students are higher than those in the control group. Can you say that your program was successful? Maybe yes; maybe no. It could be that the program is successful for the lower ability students, but is dreadfully boring for the higher ability students.

Experimental Treatment Diffusion: People will talk, and if the ideas sound interesting, they might just try to use them themselves. If the treatment group is in proximity to the control group, it is possible that the control group subjects might learn about the independent variable and begin using some of the ideas themselves.

Example: Teachers might hear about a unique approach in the staff lounge and try it, not being aware that they are part of a study. This would cloud the effect of the treatment. The researcher should conduct observations of selected classes to determine if the control group has become contaminated, and also conduct interviews with the subjects to determine their perceptions of what they were doing. Wilson and Sindelar (1991) addressed this problem by assigning subjects to treatment groups by school, so that within-school contamination would be avoided.

Compensatory Rivalry by the Control Group: Some individuals who think that their traditional way of doing things is being threatened by a new approach may try extra hard to prove that their way of doing things is best.

Example: This threat is also known as the John Henry effect, based on the folktale of the railroad worker who was pitted against a machine. John Henry wanted to prove that man was superior to the machine, so he tried extra hard. He did beat the machine—and then he died. (Let this be a warning to the control group.) (The researcher should also be aware that control groups can sometimes become disgruntled or demoralized because they are not chosen for the "new" program, and actually perform worse than normal.)

Design Considerations and Internal Validity

Beirne-Smith's (1991) study demonstrated the use of experimental design to control internal threats to validity. By the use of randomly assigned experimental and control groups, she was able to control the effects of history, maturation, testing, instrumentation, and differential selection. Her use of a pretest provided insights into initial characteristics of the subjects and thus controlled for the effects of experimental mortality (i.e., she would know the characteristics of the subjects who dropped out of her study and could compare them to those who completed it, if necessary).

External Validity or Generalizability

External validity is the extent to which findings in one study can be applied to another situation (Borg & Gall, 1989). If the findings from one study are observed in another situation, then the results are said to be generalizable or externally valid. The concept of population validity (i.e., to whom you can generalize the results) is described in Chapter 5. Bracht and Glass (1968) described another type of external validity, termed ecological validity, which concerns the extent to which the results of an experiment can be generalized, from the set of environmental conditions created by the researcher, to other environmental conditions.

Threats to Ecological Validity

Explicit Description of the Experimental Treatment: The independent variable must be sufficiently described so that the reader could reproduce it. This a common criticism of special education research, particularly as it applies to mainstreaming.
Example: Asking the question: "Is mainstreaming effective?" is really absurd without more definition, because there are so many ways that mainstreaming can be implemented.

Multiple-Treatment Interference: If subjects receive more than one treatment, then it is not possible to say which of the treatments, or which combination of the treatments, is necessary to bring about the desired result.

Example: Heward and Eachus (1979) tried to improve the writing of students who were deaf by using teacher feedback, peer tutoring, and reinforcements. It is not possible to separate the effect of these three treatments. This is a common problem now as schools implement multiple reforms to integrate students with disabilities into their neighborhood schools.

Hawthorne Effect: The idea of receiving special attention, of being singled out to participate in the study, may be enough motivation to change behavior.

Example: The Hawthorne effect derives from a study at the Western Electric Company (Roethlisberger & Dickson, 1939) of changes in light intensity and other working conditions on the workers' productivity. The researchers found that it did not matter if they increased or decreased the light intensity, the workers' productivity increased.

Novelty and Disruption Effects: A new treatment may produce positive results simply because it is novel, or the opposite may be true. A new treatment may not be effective initially because it causes a disruption in normal activities, but once it is assimilated into the system, it could become quite effective.

Example: In total inclusion schools, teachers and administrators often express a high degree of concern over the implications of having children with severe disabilities in their "regular" education classes. This concern can have a deleterious effect on the success of the inclusion program, quite apart from the actual strategies being used in the inclusion process.

Experimenter Effect: The effectiveness of a treatment may depend on the specific individual who administers it (e.g., the researcher or the teacher). The effect would not generalize to other situations because that individual would not be there.

Example: This can be a problem when volunteer teachers are used in the study because they may be selected due to their willingness to accept students with disabilities in their classes.

Pretest/Posttest Sensitization: Subjects who take a pretest or posttest may perform differently from students who never take pretests or posttests. Students who take a pretest may be more sensitized to the treatment than individuals who experience the treatment without taking a pretest. This is especially true for pretests that ask the subjects to reflect upon and express their attitudes toward a phenomenon.

Example: Students in regular classrooms might be asked, prior to a study of peer tutoring for students with disabilities, "How do you feel about working with students who have disabilities?"

Posttest sensitization is similar to pretest sensitization in that simply taking a posttest can influence a subject's response to the treatment. Taking a test can help the subject bring the information into focus in a way that subjects who do not take the test will not experience.

Other Threats to Validity

Two other threats to validity deserve mention here because of their prevalence in special education research because individualization and modifications are part of the special education culture. The first is *treatment fidelity,* in which the implementor of the independent variable (e.g., a teacher, counselor, or administrator) fails to follow the exact procedures specified by the investigator for administering the treatments (Borg & Gall, 1989). Researchers should try to maximize treatment fidelity by providing proper training and supervision, and to assess it by observations or teachers' logs. Wilson and Sindelar (1991) trained their teachers in five 1-hour sessions over 2 weeks prior to the study. The teachers had to score more than 80% on three demonstrations by acting out the part of the instructor. Also, both scripts for the lessons and prescribed examples were provided.

The second problem concerns the *strength of the experimental treatment.* An experiment to determine the effectiveness of an innovative teaching strategy can last for a few hours, days, weeks, months, or years. It is not reasonable to expect that students' learning and attitudes can be impacted by an experiment of short duration. This does not mean that the approach is not effective, but simply that it was not tried long enough. Change with special education students is often slow. Usually students in need of special education services are identified because they are progressing slowly. Measures must be sensitive to small changes and be taken over long time periods to show effects.

Challenges to Using Experimental Designs
in Special Education

Special education students are very heterogeneous, as are the settings in which they receive services. Many challenges face the special education researcher who would like to use an experimental design. Several of these factors are discussed in Chapter 5, including the distribution of students, school policies restricting differential treatment, difficulty in identifying appropriate comparison groups, small sample sizes, sampling bias, and ethical considerations. Feminists and other qualitative researchers have raised questions about the ethics of depriving one group of subjects (the control group) of a treatment that is expected to have positive effects (Guba & Lincoln, 1989; Reinharz, 1992). Because of these problems, some researchers have turned to single subject designs (described in this chapter) and qualitative designs (see Chapter 4).

QUESTIONS FOR CRITICALLY ANALYZING EXPERIMENTAL, QUASI-EXPERIMENTAL, AND SINGLE-GROUP DESIGNS

Internal Validity

1. *History.* Could events (other than your independent variable) have influenced the results?

2. *Maturation.* Could biological or psychological changes in your subjects (other than those associated with your independent variable) have influenced the results?

3. *Testing.* Could the subjects have become "test-wise" because of the pretest?

4. *Instrumentation.* Was there a difference between the pretests and posttests?

5. *Statistical regression.* Were extreme groups used?

6. *Differential selection.* Did the experimental and control groups differ in ways other than exposure to the independent variable?

7. *Experimental mortality.* Did subjects drop out during the study?

8. *Experimental treatment diffusion.* Were the treatment and control groups close enough to share ideas?

9. *Compensatory rivalry by the control group.* Did the control group try extra hard? (Were they disgruntled or demoralized?)

External Validity (Ecological Validity)
(See also, Chapter 5: Population Validity)

1. Was the experimental treatment described in sufficient detail?
2. Were multiple treatments used? Did they interfere with each other?
3. Was the Hawthorne effect operating?
4. Was the treatment influenced by being novel or disruptive?
5. What was the influence of the individual experimenter?
6. Were the subjects sensitized by taking a pretest or posttest?

Other Criteria

1. Were steps taken to insure the treatment was implemented as planned?
2. What was the influence of the strength of the treatment?
3. Was it ethical to deny the treatment to the control group?

CAUSAL COMPARATIVE AND CORRELATIONAL RESEARCH

The principal announced to the faculty that the school would participate in a research study to compare the effect of a new strategy for teaching reading to deaf and hearing students. In order to control for differential selection effects, all the names of the students in the school would be put in a hat, and then randomly assigned to the deaf and hearing groups. Of course, this example is absurd. You can't assign people to different hearing level conditions. There are many characteristics of individuals that are not manipulable, such as disabling conditions, gender, ethnicity, and age.

When studying such characteristics, a researcher can use a *causal comparative* or *correlational* approach. These types of research are quite common in special education research because of the frequency of comparison of persons with disabilities and persons without disabilities. While both approaches explore cause-and-effect relationships among variables, neither involves the experimental manipulation of treatment variables, and therefore the results cannot be used as proof of a cause-and-effect relationship. For example, blind children were compared with sighted children for their ability to identify vocal expressions of emotion (Minter, Hobson, & Pring, 1991). When the researchers found that the sighted children were more successful in correctly identifying the emotions, they did not conclude that blindness causes an inability to recognize emotions. Rather, they explored alternative (competing) explanations, such as cognitive differences, age, and time spent in residential schooling. In both types of research, it is important not to assume causality, and to explore alternative hypotheses for explaining the study's results.

The main difference procedurally between causal comparative and correlational research is in the way the independent variable is operationalized and the choice of statistic for analysis. In causal comparative research, the researcher makes group comparisons (e.g., hearing vs. deaf) and thus, typically uses *t*-tests, some variation of an analysis of variance, or nonparametric statistics. Correlational research provides an estimate of the magnitude of a relationship between two variables (e.g., relationship between degree of hearing loss and academic achievement), and therefore uses correlational statistics. Because causal comparative research compares the performance of two (or more) intact groups, the threat of differential selection must be addressed. If the two groups differ significantly on characteristics other than the independent variable (i.e., presence/absence of disabling condition), then it might be other (nonexperimental) characteristics that explain the difference between the groups.

Causal Comparative Research

Meadow (1967) compared deaf children of hearing parents and deaf children of deaf parents on a number of dependent variables. She controlled group differences by two means: matching and screening. She first screened the sample to eliminate those with deaf siblings, minority group membership, secondary disabilities, deafened after the age of 2 years, and deafness resulted from maternal rubella, Rh incompatibility, or anoxia. The students from the two groups were then matched according to sex, age, IQ test score, degree of residual hearing, and family size. (Note: The reader is referred to general research methods texts regarding difficulties with matching, such as being able to match on IQ, but not more pervasive differences in family background.) When her results indicated that deaf children of deaf parents were superior to deaf children of hearing parents on intellectual, social, and communicative functioning, she did not conclude that deaf children should be born to deaf parents. Rather, she explored such competing explanations as the effects of early exposure to manual communication and parental acceptance of deafness.

In the comparison of blind and sighted children discussed previously, Minter et al. (1991) matched the children on sex and age. On the age variable, they selected sighted children who were 18 months younger than the same-sex blind children because of evidence that cognitive development of young, congenitally blind children tends to be delayed by about 18 months, compared with their sighted peers. The researchers also administered a vocabulary test to determine if there were group differences in language ability.

Correlational Research

Correlational studies can be either prediction studies or relationship studies. In prediction studies, the researcher is interested in using one or more variables (*the predictor variables*) to predict performance on one or more other variables (*the criterion variables*). For example, kindergarten test scores can be used to predict first grade test scores if there is a strong relationship between the two sets of scores. In prediction studies, it is important to be aware of any other variables that are related to performance on the criterion variable. Relationship studies usually explore the relationships between measures of different variables obtained from the same individuals at approximately the same time to gain a better understanding of factors that contribute to making up a more complex characteristic.

It is important to realize that the correlation coefficient can range between plus and minus 1.00. The closer the correlation coefficient is to plus or minus 1.00, the stronger the relationship. A positive correlation means that the two variables increase or decrease together. For example, a positive correlation might exist between age and reading skills for deaf children, meaning that older children tend to exhibit higher reading skills. A negative correlation means that the two variables differ inversely, that is, as one goes up, the other goes down. For example, reading skills may be higher for children with less severe hearing losses; that is, as hearing loss goes up, reading skills go down. If the correlation coefficient is near zero, then no relationship exists. For example, lip reading ability might be unrelated to reading skills in deaf children.

When a correlation coefficient is squared, it tells you the amount of *explained variance*. For example, Andrews and Mason (1986) found a correlation of .5 between age and posttest scores on a measure of prereading skills for young deaf children; therefore, they stated that age accounted for 25% of the posttest score variance. They also reported that race accounted for 13% of the variance on the pretest scores, but was no longer a important factor for posttest scores. In other words, black children had significantly lower scores on the pretest, but not on the posttest.

One advantage of correlational research is that several variables can be included in one study (more easily than in experimental or causal comparative designs). However, the choice of variables should be done using a theoretical framework, rather than a shotgun approach (Borg & Gall, 1989). When a number of variables are included, then more complex procedures such as multiple regression must be used for analysis.

For example, in Andrews and Mason's (1986) investigation, they studied the relationship between background characteristics, participation in a model program, and the prereading skills of young deaf children. They used previous research to identify background characteristics commonly associated with differential reading performance, including race, sex, hearing loss, breadwinner's education, breadwinner's occupation, age, number of months using manual communication, and pretest scores of prereading skills. They entered these variables into a hierarchical multiple regression analysis on the total prereading posttest scores. The background variables were entered first, in order to control for their effects, before testing the effect of the treatment. With all the other variables controlled, the treatment still had a significant effect.

The order of entry for variables in multiple regression equations is important. When the predictor variables are correlated (a situation called *collinearity*), then the amount of variance that each independent variable accounts for can change drastically with different orders of entry of the variables. While there is no "correct" method for determining the order of variables (Kerlinger, 1973), the researcher must decide on a rationale for entry. If the researcher is interested in controlling for the effects of background characteristics before testing the effects of a treatment, then it makes sense to enter the background characteristics first (as did Andrews and Mason). Then the treatment variable will explain what is left of the variance.

QUESTIONS FOR CRITICALLY ANALYZING CAUSAL COMPARATIVE AND CORRELATIONAL RESEARCH

1. Is a causal relationship assumed between the independent (predictor) variables and the dependent (response) variable? What unexpected or

uncontrollable factors might have influenced the results? What competing explanations are explored?

2. How comparable are the groups in causal comparative studies?

3. Could a third variable cause both the independent (predictor) and dependent (criterion) variables?

4. After the initial groups were defined, were subgroup analyses conducted, based on age, sex, socioeconomic status (SES), or similar variables?

5. For correlational studies, what was the rationale for choosing and entering predictor variables? What was the percent of variance explained by the predictor variables?

6. If a predictive relationship was studied, was the test the only criterion used to select subjects? Would combining the test with other screening criteria improve its predictive validity? (A predictive validity coefficient of about .8 is needed for an accurate prediction.)

7. What is the reliability of the criterion variable (as compared to the test used to make the prediction)? Is there a restricted range for the criterion variable?

SINGLE-SUBJECT RESEARCH

Single-subject research is an experimental technique where one subject (or a small number) is studied intensively. Specifics on how to design and conduct such research can be found in Barlow and Hersen (1984), Bullis and Anderson (1986), Odom (1988), and Tawney and Gast (1984). Two basic types of single-subject designs will be discussed here: withdrawal and multiple baseline designs.

Withdrawal Designs or A-B-A-B

Withdrawal designs are based on the logic that if you can establish consistency in behavior before an intervention (A), then any change in behavior after the intervention is probably due to the treatment (B). In order to test that inference, the treatment is then withdrawn (A), the behavior is observed to determine if there is a change in the direction of the original baseline, and then the treatment is reinstated (B).

For example, Heward and Eachus (1979) designed a study that utilized the withdrawal design to teach deaf students how to use adjectives in their writing. They defined the independent variable as an instructional package that included modeling, reinforcement, and remedial feedback. The dependent variable was the correct use of adjectives in a sentence, and was operationally defined as the percentage of correct sentences that contained an adjective, but did not contain an adverb. A correct sentence was defined as accurate grammatically, punctuated properly with all words spelled correctly, and appropriate conceptually. The subject's writing behavior was observed, and the correct usage of adjectives was counted during a baseline period (A) of 15 class sessions when the instructional package was not used. The instructional package was then implemented and the use of adjectives was again counted (B) for 15 class sessions. During this time, the student's use of adjectives increased dramatically. The instructional package was then withdrawn (A), and the use of adjectives decreased (not to baseline level, but less than during B). The instructional package was then reinstated (B), and the student returned to a high use of adjectives.

This is a strong design because baseline data are provided, the behavior to be measured is specific and observable, observations were made over a considerable period of time, observations were continuous and frequent, and the researcher included a withdrawal phase to demonstrate the treatment's effectiveness.

Multiple Baseline Designs

Sometimes it is not possible to withdraw a treatment because of ethical reasons, or to observe a change in behavior after the treatment is withdrawn, because a skill has been learned or an attitude has changed which cannot be unlearned by removing a treatment. Under these conditions, researchers have turned to multiple baseline designs. There are three types: *across behaviors, across subjects,* and *across situations.*

Multiple Baseline Across Behaviors. In this design, the researcher chooses two different behaviors (e.g., writing adjectives and writing adverbs) to target for change. A baseline is established for both behaviors, then an intervention is implemented for the first behavior. If a change is observed in that behavior, then the intervention is applied to the second behavior. This is what happened in the Heward and Eachus (1979) study. The subject, who had been increasing her usage of adjectives under the treatment, began to increase her usage of adverbs also. This gives added credibility to the inference that the treatment is effective.

Multiple Baseline Across Subjects. In this design, the researchers use one behavior and try to establish a change using the same independent variable with more than one subject. Again, in the Heward and Eachus study, they implemented the treatment with four subjects, thus replicating their results.

Multiple Baseline Across Situations. In this design, the researcher chooses one behavior, one independent variable, and one subject, and attempts to change that subject's behavior in two or more situations. For example, if you have a subject who does not complete her homework in math and reading, you can choose completion of homework as the target behavior. The independent variable might be the use of token reinforcements for every day of homework completion. You would establish baseline for both behaviors, then implement the treatment for homework completion in reading class. Once a change in behavior has been observed and stabilized, the treatment can be implemented in the math class.

QUESTIONS FOR CRITICALLY ANALYZING SINGLE-SUBJECT DESIGNS

1. Does the researcher repeat the procedure with three or four subjects with similar results? Can the effect be attributed to the uniqueness of the subject?
2. Is the behavior specific and observable? (e.g., self-concept and anxiety are too broadly defined, although they can be operationalized in a specific, observable way).
3. Does the researcher provide baseline data?
4. Did the author investigate the reversal effect, that is, the removal of the treatment and return to baseline behavior? Did the researcher then reinstate the treatment and observe improved behavior? (Note: It is not always possible to reverse a learned behavior; therefore, the researcher may choose to use a multiple baseline design as an alternative.)
5. Is a series of observations made over some period of time in order to determine both the degree and direction of change?
6. Are the observations as continuous and frequent as possible?

SURVEY RESEARCH

Survey research can be thought of as either a method of data collection that can be used with other research designs (e.g., causal comparative or correlational designs), or a descriptive research design in itself. Because of the design issues related to survey research, we chose to discuss this approach to research in the quantitative methods chapter, rather than in the data collection chapter. (It should be noted that surveys that collect qualitative data by such means as records review or interviews are discussed in the qualitative methods chapter.)

Survey research has the advantage of allowing the researcher to collect information from a large number of people, in contrast to experimental research, in which the size of the sample is usually more limited. Survey research can be associated with disadvantages if it relies on self-report or reports of uninformed proxies, is retrospective, or suffers from response bias from poorly worded questions. We do not attempt to teach the reader how to design a survey research study here, because many good texts are available for that purpose (see Borg & Gall, 1989; Fowler, 1993). Rather, we concentrate on such issues related to survey research with special populations as who to collect data from, how to do it, design considerations, and response rate.

Two major surveys involving children and youths with disabilities serve as examples of conducting research with special education populations. First, the National Longitudinal Transition Study of Special Education Students (NLTS) is being conducted by SRI International for the Office of Special Education Programs, U. S. Department of Education (DeStefano & Wagner, 1991). It is a 5-year, congressionally mandated study of more than 8,000 youths, who were ages 13 to 21, and special education students in the 1985-1986 school year in more than 300 school districts and 25 state-supported schools nationwide. The NLTS describes the experiences of youths in 11 federal disability categories in the domains of secondary and postsecondary education, employment, and personal independence. DeStefano and Wagner provide excellent insights into conducting national survey research with special populations. A discussion of strategies for operationalizing outcome measures is included in Chapter 6 of this text.

Second, the Annual Survey of Hearing Impaired Children and Youth is conducted by Gallaudet University's Center for Assessment and Demographic Studies. Data collected by the survey include demographic, audiological, and educationally related information about the students, and program information about the schools they attend (Schildroth & Hotto, 1991). The 1990-91 Annual Survey data base contains information on 40,518 school-age children (ages 6 to 21), reported as attending either a residential school for deaf students, a day school for deaf students, or a local school (public or private) designed to serve hearing students (Allen, 1992).

Sources of Information

When you conduct a survey, you can collect information from the subjects themselves, from another person (such as a parent or responsible adult), or by examining records (such as a student's file). Your choice of information source depends on the nature of the person's disabling condition and the type of information you are collecting (DeStefano & Wagner, 1991). If the child has moderate to severe disabilities, it may be necessary to ask the parent or responsible adult for the information (or, in the case of deaf students, use a qualified interpreter). When youths are still in school, the parent/responsible adult may be the best source of information, because they still have frequent contact with the child. The type of information also influences the choice of information source. For example, parents would most likely be aware of whether their older child is employed and what type of job he or she has. They may even be aware of how much the child is being paid; however, parents are a less reliable source for attitudinal information such as the child's satisfaction with the job.

School records can provide good information in some instances, such as what classes the child actually took. For example, DeStefano and Wagner (1991) reported that parents may not be aware that their child took vocational training, though it is reflected on the school record. On the other hand, school records reflect a sizeable number of students who cannot be accounted for in terms of school completion. Such students are typically reported as "withdrawn," "moved," or "status unknown." Students in these categories accounted for more than 13% of secondary school leavers with disabilities in the 1986-1987 school year (U. S. Department of Education, 1989). Even parents can be confused by what constitutes graduation from high school. The NLTS revealed that 60% of parents whose children had "aged out" reported that their children had graduated (DeStefano & Wagner, 1991).

Data Collection Methods

In survey research, the researcher has a choice of mail, telephone, personal interviews, or a combination of these as a method of collecting data. Which method is used depends on the nature of the data collected, cost factors, and the size and characteristics of the sample. The NLTS relied mainly on telephone interviews, with brief written questionnaires for respondents without telephone numbers (DeStefano & Wagner, 1991). Written questionnaires will be used in later stages to solicit information from deaf youths who do not participate in the telephone interviews. In-person interviews were conducted to supplement telephone interviews in areas with high rates of nonresponse.

Bowe (1991) adapted the mail survey method for use with blind subjects. He sent the questionnaire to the subjects and then telephoned, asking them to arrange for a sighted reader's assistance, or to use a magnifying glass to read the print. He achieved a 49% response rate using this method. Freeman, Goetz, Richards, and Groenveld (1991) also conducted a survey with blind subjects, but they used a lengthy individual interview that was 15 pages long, in a semistructured format. They reported an 85% response rate and an interesting response to the methodology:

> Nearly every interviewee told us they welcomed the opportunity that the intensive semistructured interview offered them to share information and feelings, often for the first time. . . . It is doubtful that responses to a written questionnaire or standardized test scores (while useful) would have generated similar results. (p. 369)

Design Considerations

In survey research, the researcher has a choice from among simple descriptive, cross-sectional, and longitudinal approaches. The simple descriptive approach is a one-shot survey for the purpose of describing the characteristics of a sample. The cross-sectional design involves examining the responses of different groups of subjects at one point in time (e.g., first, third, and fifth grade students). Longitudinal designs survey one group or cohort of subjects at different points in time (e.g., 1 year after leaving school, 2 years, and 3 years). Cross-sectional designs have the advantage of collecting information in a shorter time frame. The disadvantage is that the experience of the students who are now in the fifth grade may have been different in the first grade, as compared to students who are now in first grade. The advantage of longitudinal research is that it follows the same (or highly similar) subjects over a period of time. The disadvantage is that it takes a long time to do it, and conditions may not be the same for students who are graduating 3 years later. Short of a time warp, there is no easy solution to these problems, other than acknowledging the limitations of individual studies.

In longitudinal research in special education, it is important to be aware that progression from one grade to another may not be the most appropriate way to measure passage of time. The students' Individual Education Plans often define goals for individual growth rather than progression from grade to grade; thus longitudinal research with these populations would more appropriately focus on age, rather than grade.

Response Rates

In survey research, a response rate is calculated based on the number of completed questionnaires or interviews, as compared to the number that were initially distributed or attempted. For example, Freeman et al. (1991) had phone numbers for 81 subjects and completed interviews with 69 subjects, for a response rate of 85%. In follow-up studies in special education, response rates range from 27% to 91%, with a reasonable expectation of 50% (Bruininks & Thurlow, 1988). Many factors affect response rate; but particularly in special education, the nature and severity of the youths' disability is a factor. DeStefano and Wagner (1991) reported a lower response rate for subjects with milder disabilities, and recommended pilot testing instruments and procedures as a way to increase response rates; that is, try out the questionnaire with a small sample to be sure it is appropriate for that audience.

Response rate is influenced by the ability to locate respondents and obtain data (DeStefano & Wagner, 1991). When subjects are in school, there is not much of a problem. Once the child has left school, there can be a problem trying to locate people through school records. Some schools do not record parents' names or students' telephone numbers, or they require parental consent to reveal students' names in special education. Sometimes you can use community agencies to locate individuals with moderate to severe disabilities, or locate them through student-friend networks, community colleges, adult education programs, former teachers, or neighborhood canvasses. When planning a longitudinal study, Edgar (1988) recommended getting permission to maintain contact before the student leaves school; obtaining the student's Social

Security number, and names and addresses of extended family members and close friends; and maintaining periodic contact with the students or the family. Response rate influences the generalizability of the findings, in that there may be a systematic bias in terms of those who do not respond to the survey. It is important in survey research to conduct a followup of a sample of nonrespondents to determine how they differ from respondents. This can be done using school records in terms of background characteristics, or by conducting a limited telephone interview with a small sample of nonrespondents, for example, 10%. These differences, if any, should be reported as part of the limitations of the study.

QUESTIONS FOR CRITICALLY ANALYZING SURVEY RESEARCH

1. Are biased questions asked (e.g., leading questions, questions that give a clue to the right or desired response)?

2. What was the influence of self-reporting on the survey? (With self-report, the subject tells you only what he or she wants you to know. Omissions or distortions can occur.)

3. What was the response rate? Was a followup done of nonrespondents? Were they similar to or different from respondents?

4. Does the researcher ask too many questions and thus impose an unreasonable burden on the respondent?

5. What is the effect of the type of options provided (e.g., free response, closed-end questions, "happy" faces)?

6. If the desired respondent was not available, who answered the survey? Adequacy of proxies?

7. How were answers recorded (e.g., taped, notes, self-report)?

8. If interviewers were used, were they trained?

9. Was the survey cross-sectional or longitudinal? If cross-sectional, what is the effect of different students at each grade level?

QUESTIONS AND ACTIVITIES FOR DISCUSSION AND APPLICATION

1. For the following study:
   a. identify the research approach that is used
   b. identify the independent and dependent variables

c. draw the design that was used

d. critique the study, using the appropriate criteria

The auditory preferences of autistic children were compared to those of normally developing and mentally retarded children by allowing them to choose between their mothers' speech and the noise of superimposed voices (a sound effect obtained in a busy canteen) (Klin, 1991). The groups of mentally retarded and normally developing children showed a stronger preference for their mothers' speech than did the autistic children. The author suggests that this abnormal reaction to speech is a feature of autistic children's overall disregard for people. But she explored such competing explanations as the specific auditory properties of the stimuli or the children's receptive language abilities. She concludes: "If, however, the present findings are substantiated, the issue of whether the lack of attraction to speech sounds is a *feature* of, or a *contributory factor* to, autistic children's overall social unresponsiveness, will have to be examined" (p. 39). Thus, Klin is recognizing the limitations of her study, in that she does not conclude that autism causes an aversion to people.

2. For the following study:

a. identify the research approach that was used

b. critique the study, using the appropriate criteria

Pollard and Oakland (1985) examined the relationship between 15 family, psychological, and demographic variables and reading and math achievement for deaf children at a residential school. The variables were chosen because they "were thought to represent important child-related characteristics which may have had some influence on children's academic development" (p. 69). No previous research or theoretical framework was used as a rationale for the inclusion of variables related to math or reading achievement. For math achievement, the significant predictors were IQ and size of weekly allowance (a proxy for socioeconomic status). The research basically told us that children with higher IQs and from higher SES homes achieve higher in math. This study is an example of the shotgun approach that entered variables into the equation without controlling for background characteristics first.

3. Critique the following study, using the questions for critically analyzing survey research:

Shapiro and Lentz (1991) adapted the survey research methods for use with a sample with learning disabilities. They first contacted their subjects by telephone to tell them that a survey was coming, then mailed the survey. They then recontacted the subjects by telephone, interviewing them while they had the survey in front of them. They were able to get an 88% response rate 6 months after graduation, and a 72% response rate for 12- and 24-month followups.

4. For the following studies:
   a. identify the research approach that was used
   b. critique the study, using the appropriate criteria

STUDY #1: Winterling (1990) taught vocabulary words to a subject who was mentally disabled. He used three different word lists, thereby showing that the treatment was effective on the learning of different words in the same subject.

STUDY #2: Winterling (1990) used a multiple baseline, across-subjects design by expanding his treatment for teaching vocabulary words to three subjects with mental disabilities or learning disabilities.

4

Qualitative Methods

The researcher observed mainstreaming programs for deaf youths at the elementary, middle, and high school levels, operated by the local school district, for 2 years to investigate how deaf and hearing youths were educated together (Higgins, 1992). He observed in self-contained and mainstream classes, in the cafeteria, and on the playground. He talked with the principal, administrators, teachers, other staff, parents, and students, and he read about other programs. This example illustrates the approach of qualitative methods in special education.

In This Chapter

- The importance of qualitative methods in special education research is explored.
- Types of qualitative methods are discussed, along with methodological implications in special education of the philosophical assumptions of this approach to research.
- Data collection strategies for qualitative research in special education are introduced.
- Questions for critically analyzing qualitative research are provided.

IMPORTANCE OF QUALITATIVE METHODS IN SPECIAL EDUCATION RESEARCH

Patton (1990) suggested using qualitative methods under the following conditions:

1. the program emphasizes individualized outcomes
2. detailed, in-depth information is needed about certain clients or programs
3. the focus is on diversity among, idiosyncrasies of, and unique qualities exhibited by individuals

Table 4.1

Examples of Quantitative and Qualitative Subject Descriptions

---

In a quantitative survey study, the subjects were described as follows:

> "These children were identified as learning disabled in accordance with criteria (which closely resembles the federal criteria) set forth by the Delaware Department of Public Instruction" (Bear, Clever, & Proctor, 1991, p. 414).

In a qualitative study, the description read:

> One student . . . "had a reading deficit. He had a tough time decoding words, although his spelling and writing were pretty good. He always seemed to understand what he had read, but if he had to read material, he struggled, slowly, missing key vocabulary words" (Davis & Ferguson, 1992, p. 126).

---

4. no standardized instrument is available that can validly and reliably measure program outcomes

Many of the criteria that establish the appropriateness of choosing qualitative methods parallel the conditions in special education.

In special education, low incidence conditions, such as deaf-blindness, cause sample sizes to be either restricted or small. This issue is discussed in Chapter 5, on the identification and selection of subjects. In special education, the subjects are unique, with diversity across categories of disabilities as well as within them. Two descriptions of students in quantitative and qualitative studies (as presented in Table 4.1) demonstrate the difference in focus for these two types of studies. Qualitative studies tend to provide more detail about the uniqueness of the students' disabling conditions than do quantitative studies.

In special education, each student's program, by definition, is deliberately designed to be unique in order to satisfy that student's needs. This is reflected in the requirements of the Individuals with Disabilities Education Act (IDEA), including an Individualized Education Plan (IEP) for school-age students, an Individual Family Service Plan (IFSP) for children from birth through 3 years old, and an Individual Transition Plan (ITP) required for all individuals by their 16th birthday. By definition, if not by legal mandate, the programs for special education students are diverse and idiosyncratic.

Peck and Furman (1992) explored the importance of qualitative research in special education in terms of recent developments in the philosophy of science, the need for more holistic analysis of problems in policy and practice, and increased attention to descriptions of the world, as experienced by individuals, in the analysis of issues in special education. They identified several substantive contributions that qualitative research has made to special education.

First, qualitative researchers have identified the fundamental roles of ideology, organizational dynamics, and the social/political process in shaping policy and practice in special education. Peck and Furman's analysis suggests that the most fundamental problems constraining the inclusion of children with disabilities in regular classes are less technical than political in nature. Therefore, focusing on the instructional process affecting children's behavior is less appropriate than addressing political issues. They contend that adherence to the positivist tradition of research is likely to lead researchers away from asking some critical questions about why children with disabilities are not succeeding in school. This ability to provide insight into the social/political process is one that has been emphasized by feminists as well (Reinharz, 1992).

Second, Peck and Furman noted the value of constructing some sense of the insider's view. They noted that qualitative research has enabled the development of professional interventions in special education that are responsive to the cognitive and motivational interpretations of the world held by children, parents, and professionals. For example, definitions of aberrant or inappropriate behaviors can be reframed in terms of their functional meaning for a child.

Third, qualitative methods have led to insights into the cultural values, institutional practices, and interpersonal interactions that influence special education practice. For example, placement and categorizing children in special education are subject to these influences, and can be understood only through a research process that can look at different levels of social ecology.

TYPES OF QUALITATIVE RESEARCH

Many different types of qualitative research are practiced in educational research. In fact, Tesch (1990) identified 26 different types in her analysis. In an attempt to simplify and provide a broad organizing framework to describe types of qualitative research, Langenbach, Vaughn, and Aagaard (1994) narrowed "perspective-seeking" approaches to research into two main categories: ethnography and phenomenology. Langenbach et al. recognized that this dichotomy represented an over-simplification of a complex set of practices, and that differences exist within these categories. They combined interpretivism and ethnography as one category, and phenomenology and artistic approaches as the second. (Note: Qualitative methods can also be used within the positivist paradigm, for example, if the researcher establishes predetermined, static questions to guide the research, and/or converts the qualitative data to frequency counts and so on. However, we focus on the use of qualitative methods within the constructivist tradition, because of the unique criteria for judging quality associated with such research.)

Examples of the phenomenological approach in special education could study what the experience of being in a total inclusion classroom is like, or what the experience of being a student with a disability (or one without a disability) in an integrated classroom is like. In contrast, an ethnographic approach to special education research could include investigating the impact of a program designed to facilitate integration of students with disabilities, or studying the culture of the total inclusion classroom, or interactions among children with or without disabilities.

Phenomenological research differs from ethnographic approaches in its emphasis on the individual, and on subjective experience (Tesch, 1990). It seeks the individual's perceptions and meaning of a phenomenon or experience. Typically, phenomenological research asks: What is the participant's experience like? The intent is to understand and describe an event from the point of view of the participant. The feature that distinguishes phenomenological research from other qualitative research approaches is that the subjective experience is at the center of the inquiry.

Tesch (1990) identified ethnography as the most common type of qualitative method used in educational research. Ethnography can be defined as a research method designed to describe and analyze practices and beliefs of cultures and communities. For example, Keller, Karp, and Carlson (1993) and Mertens (1992) studied community and school contexts for the integration of students with disabilities in total inclusion programs in their neighborhood schools.

The case study is one type of ethnographic (interpretive) approach that involves intensive and detailed study of one individual, or of a group as an entity, through observation, self-reports, and any other means (Langenbach et al., 1994; Tesch, 1990). Because of the emphasis on the individual, case studies have played a very important role in special education research. The reader interested in this methodology is encouraged to read Yin's *Case Study Research* (1989) and *Applications of Case Study Research* (1993). Examples of case studies in special education can be found in Koppenhaver and Yoder's (1992) literature review of case studies related to individuals with physical disabilities, and Ferguson's (1992) case study of six students with severe autism.

PHILOSOPHICAL ASSUMPTIONS AND METHODOLOGICAL IMPLICATIONS IN SPECIAL EDUCATION RESEARCH

First, the constructivist paradigm purports that reality is created as a result of a process of social construction; that is, there is no one reality that is waiting to be "discovered," as is believed in the positivist paradigm (Guba & Lincoln, 1989). For example, the concept of "disability" is a socially constructed phenomenon that means different things to different people. The methodological implication of having multiple realities is that the research questions cannot be definitively established before the study begins, rather, they will evolve and change as the study progresses. In special education research, the concept of multiple realities and social construction of reality also mean that the perceptions of a variety of types of persons must be sought. For example, Crowley (1993) used extensive interviews and classroom observations to explore multiple perspectives of practices that help or impede the learning of students with behavioral disorders in mainstream settings (including the opinions of the students themselves). Reiff, Gerber, and Ginsberg (1993) constructed a definition of learning disability from the perspective of insider-adults with learning disabilities who focused on the academic areas of reading and writing, rather than on the vocational and social dysfunctions found in many traditional definitions.

Second, the constructivist paradigm assumes that the inquirer and inquired-into are interlocked, each affecting the other through the process of their mutual interaction. Thus, the qualitative researcher rejects the notion of objectivity that is espoused by the positivist, and opts for a more interactive, personally involved style of data collection. For example, one special education teacher conducted a qualitative research study in collaboration with a university researcher, in which she discussed with her students with mild learning disabilities how they could more effectively respond to the demands in the mainstream classroom (Davis & Ferguson, 1992). She then used their ideas to structure the intervention that was the focus of her qualitative study.

Third, the constructivist believes that facts are products of social construction and therefore, the values surrounding any statement of "facts" must be explored and made explicit. The concept of least restrictive environment (LRE) in special education exemplifies the connection between facts and values. The federal government defined LRE as inclusion of students with disabilities in regular education classes as much as possible. However, deaf advocates contended that, because of communication barriers, and even with qualified interpreters, inclusion in regular education would be socially isolating and hence restrictive to deaf students.

QUALITATIVE METHODS AND DATA COLLECTION STRATEGIES

Because there is no one correct method for conducting qualitative research, Stainback and Stainback (1988) recommend that researchers describe their methodology in detail. Stainback and Stainback offer a framework for structuring and conducting a qualitative research study that provides one approach for designing and conducting such a study. The reader who intends to conduct a qualitative research study is referred to other texts that explore this topic in more depth (Bogdan & Biklen, 1992; Fetterman, 1989; Guba & Lincoln, 1989; Lincoln & Guba, 1985; Marshall & Rossman, 1989; Patton, 1990; Yin, 1989, 1993).

Typically, qualitative researchers in the constructivist paradigm use three main methods for collecting data: *participant observation, interviews,* and *document and records review.*

Participant Observation

Spradley (1980) outlined five types of participation:

1. Nonparticipation: The lowest level of involvement is usually accomplished by watching a videotape of the situation. For example, a researcher could ask a teacher to turn on a video camera at selected times when a

student with disabilities is in her class. The researcher would then review the tape at a later time.

2. Passive participation: The researcher is present, but does not interact with the participants. Keller (1993) used this approach in observing a girl with Down syndrome who was integrated in a regular education classroom.

3. Moderate participation: The researcher attempts to balance the insider/outsider roles by observing, participating in some, but not all of the activities. Keller (1993) used this approach when he taught three lessons in the sixth-grade classroom in which the girl with Down syndrome was integrated.

4. Active participation: The researcher generally does what the others do, but does not participate completely. Mertens (1991a) used this approach in a study of gifted deaf adolescents in a summer enrichment program. She was with the students all day in the classroom, on field trips, and at meals. However, she did not sleep in the students' dorms at night, and thus was not involved in their "after dark" activities.

5. Complete participation: The researcher becomes a natural participant, which has the disadvantage of trying to collect data and maintain a questioning and reflective stance. This approach was used by Ferguson, who was a special education teacher for students with learning disabilities (Davis & Ferguson, 1992). She continued with her role as the special education teacher while collecting qualitative data by observation and interviews.

Interviewing

Interviews in a qualitative study are typically done with an unstructured or minimally structured format. Interviewing can be conducted as a part of participant observation, or even as a casual conversation. The questions emerge as the researcher is sensitized to the meanings that the participants bring to the situation. As the study evolves, interviewing can become more structured and formal.

Interviewing students with disabilities can present challenges because of the capabilities or communication needs of the respondents. For example, Ferguson (1992) conducted a case study of autistic students, in which he interviewed adults who had various connections to autistic individuals at the school, including regular and special education teachers, administrators, and support staff. He commented, "Because of the limited verbal skills of the students in Mel's class, I did not conduct formal interviews with any of them. I did have short, informal conversations with the students when I was there doing observations" (p. 166).

Mertens (1991a) interviewed gifted deaf adolescents and found that it was necessary to train herself to take notes while watching the respondents in order to not miss any of their signs. She found that she could accommodate to this situation by using a clipboard that was tilted enough for her to see, with her peripheral vision, that the writing was going onto the right part of the page. She also paused between questions to finish writing each response, and then spent time immediately after each interview, filling in any holes that had been created by this interview process.

Document and Records Review

All organizations leave trails composed of documents and records that trace their history and current status. Documents and records include not only the typical paper products such as memos, reports, and plans, but also computer files, tapes (audio and video), and other artifacts. It is to these documents and records that the qualitative researcher must turn in order to get the necessary background of the situation and insights into the dynamics of everyday functioning. The researcher cannot be in all places at all times; therefore, documents and records give the researcher access to information that would otherwise be unavailable. In special education research, documents that might be important include report cards, special education files, discipline records, IEPs, IEP meeting minutes, curriculum materials, and test scores.

CRITICALLY ANALYZING
QUALITATIVE RESEARCH

Criteria for judging the quality of qualitative research that parallel the criteria for judging positivist, quantitative research have been outlined by a number of writers (Guba & Lincoln, 1989; Stainback & Stainback, 1988). Guba and Lincoln equate credibility with internal validity, transferability with external validity, dependability with reliability, and confirmability with objectivity. They added the additional category of authenticity for qualitative research. In this section, each criterion is explained, along with ways to enhance quality in special education research.

Credibility

Guba and Lincoln (1989) identified credibility as the criterion in qualitative research that parallels internal validity in positivist research. Internal validity means the attribution within the experimental situation that the independent variable caused the observed change in the dependent variable. In qualitative research, the credibility test asks if there is a correspondence between the way the respondents actually perceive social constructs and the way the researcher portrays their viewpoints. A number of research strategies can be used to enhance credibility, including:

Prolonged and Substantial Engagement. There is no hard-and-fast rule that says how long a researcher must stay at a site. When the researcher has confidence that themes and examples are repeating instead of extending, it may be time to leave the field. Keller (1993) observed the girl with Down syndrome from January through June of one year.

Persistent Observation. The researcher should observe long enough to identify salient issues. The researcher should avoid premature closure, that is, coming to a conclusion about a situation without sufficient observations. Keller (1993) had more than 80 contacts with the school or the staff over a 6-month period.

Peer Debriefing. The researcher should engage in an extended discussion, with a disinterested peer, of findings, conclusions, analysis, and hypotheses. The peer should pose searching questions to help the researcher confront his or her own values and to guide the next steps in the study. Keller (1993) shared the narratives from his field notes with two other researchers involved in the school.

Negative Case Analysis. Working hypotheses can be revised, based on the discovery of cases that do not fit; however, it should not be expected that all cases will fit the appropriate categories. Guba and Lincoln (1989) state that when a "reasonable" number of cases fit, then negative case analysis provides confidence in the hypothesis that is being proposed. For example, suppose a researcher sees a pattern emerging, which suggests that a top-down approach to a total inclusion program creates resistance in the school staff (Mertens, 1992). The researcher could seek additional data for negative case analysis from a school that used a bottom-up approach to total inclusion. If resistance was identified in that setting as well, the researcher would need to revise the emerging hypothesis that administration style *alone* creates resistance. It may be one of many factors that contribute to resistance to change.

Progressive Subjectivity. The researcher should monitor his or her developing constructions and document the process of change from the beginning of the study until it ends. The researcher can share this statement of beliefs with the peer debriefer, so that the peer can challenge the researcher who has not kept an open mind, but has only found what was expected from the beginning. For example, a study of the social experiences of deaf high school students suggested that social isolation can be a very painful result of being the only deaf student (or one of a few) in a school (Mertens, 1989). The emotional strength of this finding might have left the researcher biased against the integration of students with disabilities into regular classes. Consequently, in Mertens's subsequent work in total inclusion research (1992), she needed to discuss this personal experience at the beginning and throughout the duration of the study, so that she could keep an open mind and not be biased by previous experience.

Member Checks. This is the most important criterion in establishing credibility. The researcher must verify with the respondent groups the constructions that are developing as a result of data collected and analyzed. Member checks can be formal and informal. For example, at the end of an interview, the researcher can summarize what has been said, and ask if the notes accurately reflect the person's position. Drafts of the research report can be shared with the members for comment. Mertens (1993a) established a daily feedback loop with trainers in special education who were deaf, or blind, or had no disabilities. She discussed the data that she had collected from the previous day to clarify their perspectives and to enhance her ability to represent their viewpoints accurately.

Triangulation. Triangulation involves checking information that has been collected from different sources or methods for consistency of evidence across sources of data. Guba and Lincoln (1989) no longer support this notion of triangulation because it implies that it is possible (or desirable) to find consistency across sources, which contradicts the notion of multiple realities discussed earlier in this chapter. They say that triangulation can still be used to check on factual data (e.g., how many children are in a program), but they recommend the use of member checks for other types of data. Keller (1993) collected information by means of observations in classrooms, planning sessions, staff meetings, parent-teacher conferences, and IEP meetings. He taught three lessons in the classroom of the student in his study; he interviewed the student, her mother, and her teacher from her old school; and he held informal conversations with her regular and special education teachers and the principal. He combined the data from all of these sources to support his findings.

Transferability

Guba and Lincoln (1989) identified transferability as the qualitative parallel to external validity in positivist research. External validity means the degree to which you can generalize the results to other situations. They contend that in qualitative research, the burden of transferability is on the reader to determine the degree of similarity between the study site and the receiving context. The researcher's responsibility is to provide sufficient detail to enable the reader to make such a judgment. Extensive and careful description of the time, place, context, and culture is known as *thick description.* Mertens (1990a) studied the reasons that referrals were increasing to a special school that served several school districts in a rural area. She provided an in-depth description of the community in which the special school was located, as well as the sending and receiving schools, by means of demographic and observational data. She observed in all the schools and provided a description of the physical setup of the classrooms and the processes of instruction that were used. Thus, readers could determine how similar their own conditions were to those reported by Mertens. A thick description of the context was important because the rural nature of the community had an impact on understanding the reasons for the increased referrals (e.g., in terms of ability to attract and retain qualified special education staff, and to provide services for students with low-incidence disabilities in sparsely populated areas).

Dependability

Guba and Lincoln (1989) identified dependability as the qualitative parallel to reliability. Reliability means stability over time in the positivist paradigm. In the constructivist paradigm, change is expected, but it should be tracked and be publicly inspectable. A dependability audit can be conducted to attest to the quality and appropriateness of the inquiry process. For example, Mertens (1991a) began a study of ways to encourage gifted deaf adolescents to enter science careers, with a focus on instructional strategies used in science classes. However, emerging patterns in the data suggested the importance of examining administrative practices that facilitated the acquisition of competent interpreters or teachers and staff who were deaf. This change of focus is acceptable and to be expected in qualitative research, but it should be documented.

Confirmability

Guba and Lincoln (1989) identified confirmability as the qualitative parallel to objectivity. Objectivity means that the influence of the researcher's judgment is minimized. Confirmability means that the data and their interpretation are not figments of the researcher's imagination. Qualitative data can be tracked to its source, and the logic that is used to interpret the data should be made explicit. Guba and Lincoln recommend a confirmability audit to attest to the fact that the data can be traced to original sources, and the process of synthesizing data to reach conclusions can be confirmed. The confirmability audit can be conducted in conjunction with the dependability audit. Thus, a special education researcher's peers can review field notes, interview transcripts, and so on, and determine whether the conclusions are supported by the data (Keller, 1993).

Authenticity

Authenticity refers to the presentation of a balanced view of all perspectives, values, and beliefs (Stainback & Stainback, 1988). It answers the question: Has the researcher been fair in presenting views? Among the criteria identified by Guba and Lincoln (1989) to judge the authenticity of investigations conducted within the constructivist paradigm were the following:

Fairness answers the question: To what extent are different constructions and their underlying value structures solicited and honored in the process? In order to be fair, the researcher must identify the respondents and how information about their constructions was obtained. Conflicts and value differences should be displayed. There should also be open negotiation of the recommendations and agenda for future actions. Total inclusion research can be judged to be fair if the varying viewpoints, both for and against (and the conditions under which inclusion would be supported), are included in the report (Keller et al., 1993; Mertens, 1992).

Ontological Authenticity is the degree to which the individual's or group's conscious experience of the world became more informed or sophisticated. This can be determined based on the testimony of the respondents, or by means of an audit trail that documents changes in individuals' constructions throughout the process. In the study of increased referrals to a special school, respondents came to understand the discrepancy between policy and practice with regard to referral of students with disabilities to special schools (Mertens, 1990a). The policy said that students with disabilities should be educated as much as possible with general education students and that, as a last resort, *before* referral to a special school, they should be provided with educational services in a separate, special education classroom in their home school. Local school staff did not support use of the special education classroom because they perceived it as stigmatizing for the student to go to a separate classroom. They preferred to refer a student to the special school when they had exhausted attempts to integrate a student with a disability in a general education classroom.

Catalytic Authenticity is the extent to which action is stimulated by the inquiry process. Techniques for determining this criterion include respondent testimony, and examination of actions reported in follow-up studies. Following the completion of the study of increased referrals at the special school, the state department of education representative asked Mertens to assist in implementing the recommendations (1990a). For example, personnel from the special school began to serve as consultants to the local schools to assist them in retaining and meeting the needs of the students with disabilities prior to referral to the special school.

QUESTIONS FOR CRITICALLY ANALYZING QUALITATIVE RESEARCH

1. Did the researcher maintain sufficient involvement at the site to overcome distortions, to uncover people's constructions, and to understand the context's culture?

2. Did the researcher avoid premature closure?
3. Did the researcher use peer debriefing?
4. Did the researcher use negative case analysis?
5. Did the researcher prepare a statement of beliefs and share those with the peer debriefer?
6. Did the researcher use member checks?
7. Did the researcher use triangulation?
8. Did the researcher provide sufficient thick description?
9. Did the researcher do a dependability audit?
10. Did the researcher do a confirmability audit?
11. Did the researcher display conflicts and value differences?
12. Did the individuals and groups become more informed or sophisticated about their experiences?
13. Did the evaluation stimulate action?

QUESTIONS AND ACTIVITIES FOR DISCUSSION AND APPLICATION

1. In your opinion, why are qualitative research methods appropriate/not appropriate for special education?
2. What are the philosophical assumptions of the constructivist paradigm, and what are their methodological implications in special education?
3. Explain the main types of qualitative research, that is, ethnography and phenomenology. How are they similar/different? Give an example in special education of an application of each of these approaches.
4. Explain the three methods of collecting data that can be used in qualitative research. Give examples of how these could be applied in special education.
5. Given the following research problem, explain what the researchers could do to improve the quality of their study. Structure your answer using the following categories:
   a. credibility
   b. transferability
   c. dependability
   d. confirmability
   e. authenticity

Example: Pull-out programs (e.g., resource rooms or remedial classes) have been criticized for segregating low-achieving students, providing them with a fragmented curriculum, and allowing regular classroom teachers to avoid responsibility for meeting all the students' needs. Pull-in programs have been proposed as one alternative, where the special education or remedial teacher provides instruction in the regular classroom. This study used observations of two pull-in programs to obtain information about implementation, instructional context, and variability among classrooms implementing pull-in. Three pull-out programs taught by the same special and remedial education teachers served as comparison groups (Gelzheiser & Meyers, 1992).

6. Select a research problem in special education. Describe how you could approach it from both a quantitative and a qualitative perspective. What are the strengths and weaknesses of each approach as applied to your problem area?

5

Identification and Selection
of Subjects

*Females with disabilities who had been out of secondary school
for five years were significantly less likely than their male peers
to be employed.*

Wagner (1992)

The meaning of this statement is not clear unless the reader knows
something about the sample of individuals from which the data were
collected to make this statement. Research results are ambiguous and
difficult to interpret if the characteristics of the sample are not clear.
This problem is especially complex in special education research, in
that definitions of who is and who is not included in a disability category
are quite variable. Smith (1982) reported that only half the students who
were in special education exhibited behavior, characteristics, or test
scores that were consistent with state special education criteria. Also,
Ysseldyke, Algozzine, Shinn, and McGue (1982) reported no reliable
psychometric difference between special education and regular education students on 49 measures of cognition, perceptual motor skills,
personality or academic performance.

Clarity in describing special education populations is important for
understanding the professional literature and communicating research
results to others, and in the designing of studies (i.e., selecting samples,
measures, and so on). Researchers have a responsibility to describe fully
and clearly the characteristics of their populations and samples, and the
educational contexts in which services are provided. Although this text
focuses primarily on methods for clearly defining characteristics associated with disabilities, researchers in special education should be
aware of and report all important characteristics of the sample, including ethnicity and gender. A larger percentage of minorities and males
have traditionally been identified as needing special education services
(Graf, 1992); therefore, the researcher must be precise about issues

regarding ethnicity and gender in discussing the generalizability or transferability of a study's results.

Considerable controversy exists as to the wisdom of using labels for children with disabilities (Gage & Berliner, 1991). Proponents of labeling believe labels help identify children with special needs and help in further diagnosis and treatment, and also facilitate communication, legislation, and administration in serving exceptional students. Opponents feel that labels are misleading, allow for misdiagnosis, and encourage stereotyping instead of encouraging accurate assessment and treatment of students' needs. We feel that categories should be broad, but that they should not conceal the range and complexity of the characteristics, needs, and abilities of the students.

In This Chapter

- Conceptual and operational definitions for special education students are described for the categories included in the federal legislation (Individuals with Disabilities Education Act), as well as for several emerging areas.
- Designing and selecting samples are described in terms of three choices available to researchers: probability-based samples, purposeful samples, and volunteer samples.
- Issues specific to special education samples are discussed, such as unique characteristics associated with different disability areas, practical constraints, comparison groups, sample size, sampling error, and sampling bias.
- The topics of generalizability, transferability, external validity, ethics, and confidentiality are also included.
- Questions for critically analyzing sampling designs and procedures are provided.

TYPES OF DEFINITIONS:
CONCEPTUAL AND OPERATIONAL

Research constructs such as special education labels can be defined in two ways: Conceptual definitions are those that use other constructs to explain the meaning, and operational definitions are those that specify how the construct will be measured. For example, special education can be conceptually defined as follows:

... the term "special education" means specially designed instruction, at no cost to the parent, to meet the unique needs of a *child with disabilities*, including classroom instruction, instruction in physical education, home instruction, and instruction in hospitals and institutions. (34 Code of Federal Regulations 300.14)

When using a conceptually defined construct, the other constructs used in the definition must be defined as well, such as *at no cost, child with disabilities,* and *physical education.*

An operational definition of special education might be "services provided in schools by teachers and related service personnel who have special education certification." You could then go to a school and ask the principal to identify students who receive services from teachers and related service personnel who have special education certification. For research purposes, the conceptual definition must be accompanied by an operational definition in order to communicate to the reader what was actually done in the research.

IDENTIFICATION OF SPECIAL EDUCATION POPULATIONS

The U. S. Office of Special Education publishes an annual report to Congress that provides information on the extent to which children and youths with disabilities are receiving special education and related services (U.S. Department of Education, 1993b). They use a number of sources of information, including state reports on the annual counts of the number of children and youths with disabilities receiving special education and related services as required under the Individuals with Disabilities Education Act (IDEA), Part B and Chapter 1 of the Elementary and Secondary Education Act (ESEA), State Operated Programs (SOP).

A total of 4,994,169 children and youths (birth through age 21) with disabilities were served during school year 1991-1992 under the IDEA (Part B) and Chapter 1 (SOP) programs (U.S. Department of Education, 1993b). This represents a 3.9% increase over the 1990-1991 school year. The largest increases occurred in the categories of specific learning disabilities, speech or language impairments, and serious emotional disturbance. The 1991-1992 school year was the first time national data were collected on serving children with autism and traumatic brain injury.

Table 5.1

Students Aged 6-21 Served Under IDEA, Part B and Chapter 1 of ESEA
(SOP), by Type of Disability: School Year 1991-92

Type of disability	IDEA, Part B		Chap. 1 (SOP)		Total	
	Number	%	Number	%	Number	%
Specific learning disabilities	2,218,948	51.3	30,047	16.5	2,248,995	49.9
Speech or language impairments	990,016	22.9	10,655	5.9	1,000,671	22.2
Mental retardation	500,986	11.6	53,261	29.3	554,247	12.8
Serious emotional disturbance	363,877	8.4	36,793	20.2	400,670	8.9
Multiple disabilities	80,655	1.9	17,747	9.8	98,402	2.2
Hearing impairments	41,003	1.0	17,161	9.4	60,763	1.3
Orthopedic impairments	46,222	1.1	5,468	3.0	51,690	1.1
Other health impairments	56,401	1.3	2,479	1.4	58,880	1.3
Visual impairments	18,296	0.4	5,873	3.2	24,169	0.5
Deaf-blindness	773	0.0	650	0.4	1,423	0.0
Autism	3,555	0.1	1,653	0.9	5,208	0.1
Traumatic brain injury	285	0.0	45	0.0	330	0.0
All conditions	4,323,704	100.0	181,744	100.0	4,505,448	99.8

SOURCE: U.S. Department of Education, 1993b

IDEA includes 12 categories of special education populations that are eligible for federal funding. Frequencies of occurrence for these 12 categories for students ages 6-21 are presented in Table 5.1. (Children are counted by their specific disability only for ages 6-21). For each population, we present the federal conceptual definition; an operational definition; and characteristics relevant to research design. Following a description of these 12 populations, a discussion is presented of other categories, such as infant and toddler special populations, developmentally delayed, and at-risk populations.

Specific Learning Disability

The federal regulations provide the following conceptual definition of learning disability:

"Specific learning disability" means a disorder in one or more of the basic psychological processes involved in understanding or in using language, spoken or written, which may manifest itself in an imperfect ability to listen, think, speak, read, write, spell, or to do mathematical calculations. The term includes such conditions as perceptual impairments, brain injury, minimal brain disfunction, dyslexia, and developmental aphasia. The term does not include children who have learning problems which are primarily the result of visual, hearing, or motor impairments, mental retardation, emotional disturbance or environmental, cultural, or economic disadvantage. (34 Code of Federal Regulations 300.5 (a))

The ambiguity of the definition of learning disabilities has led to many classification problems. For example, using the existing classification system, 85% of normal children could be classified as LD, 88% of low-functioning students could be classified as LD, and 4% of LD students did not meet the criteria for such a placement (Ysseldyke, Algozzine, & Epps, 1983).

The federal regulations did offer the following operational definition of learning disabilities: an ability-achievement discrepancy, existing in spite of the provision of age appropriate instruction, not caused primarily by other conditions (U.S. Department of Health, Education, and Welfare, 1977, Section 121a.541). (Note: The "other conditions" referred to above include those specifically excluded in the definition of learning disabilities, that is, learning problems primarily the result of visual, hearing, or motor impairments, mental retardation, emotional disturbance, economic disadvantage, or sensory or physical impairment.)

Despite this operational definition, controversy continues to surround the definition of learning disabilities for three reasons (Bennett & Ragosta, 1988). First, disorders that comprise learning disabilities are poorly conceptualized; for example, minimal brain dysfunction, perceptual disability, and dyslexia all refer to conditions whose etiology, symptoms, prevalence, and treatment are uncertain (Reid & Hresko, 1981). Second, the definition requires an ability-achievement discrepancy not the result of other factors, such as mental retardation, emotional disturbance, economic disadvantage, or sensory or physical impairment. This assumes that you can reliably differentiate causes of school failure. Third, learning disability is built on the idea of underachievement, and thus assumes that potential can be measured. In reality, tests can only predict future achievement, from which potential is inferred. Also, underachievement is not peculiar to children with learning disabilities.

The population with learning disabilities is very heterogeneous. Shepard, Smith, and Vojir (1983) identified four major groups within the learning disabled students in Colorado, with 18 distinct subgroups. Despite this heterogeneity, certain general characteristics about the learning disabled population have been noted which have implications for research (Bennett & Ragosta, 1988). Poor basic skills, particularly in reading, may prevent accurate assessment of higher level abilities as well as impede assessment of other skills that are dependent on text reading.

Speech or Language Impairments

The federal regulations provide the following conceptual definition of speech or language impairments:

> "Speech or language impairments" means a communication disorder such as stuttering, impaired articulation, a language impairment, or a voice impairment, which adversely affects a child's educational performance. (34 Code of Federal Regulations 300.5 (a))

Educators tend to separate speech and language disorders. Speech disorders are those that deviate so far from the speech of other people that they call attention to themselves, interfere with communication, or cause the speaker or listener to be distressed (Gage & Berliner, 1991). For example, speech disorders include problems with articulation (omissions, substitutions, distortions, additions of sounds), voice (pitch, loudness, quality), and fluency (stuttering). Language disorders are those that arise in the basic understanding of the symbols we use to convey ideas (e.g., delayed language development and aphasia, that is, difficulty in comprehending or formulating messages).

Mental Retardation

The conceptual definition of mental retardation provided in the federal regulations states:

> "Mental retardation" means significantly subaverage general intellectual functioning existing concurrently with deficits in adaptive behavior and manifested during the developmental period, which adversely affects a child's educational performance. (34 Code of Federal Regulation 300.5 (a))

Operational definitions of mental retardation vary by state, but a definition based solely on IQ is not adequate because of the construct of adaptive behavior. Adaptive behavior includes sensorimotor, communication, self-help, socialization, daily living, and vocational skills. Adaptive behavior can be assessed by tests such as the Vineland Social Maturity Scale or the Adaptive Behavior Scale. (Note: For sources of additional information about the tests used in special education, the reader is referred to Chapter 6.)

Three levels of mental retardation have been operationally defined as subaverage performance on a measure of adaptive behavior and IQ measured in the following ranges with the Wechsler Intelligence Scale for Children-Revised (WISC-R) (Gage & Berliner, 1991; Heward & Orlansky, 1988):

Category of mental retardation	IQ Range
Educable mentally retarded	55-69
Trainable mentally retarded	40-54
Severe to profound mentally retarded	39 and below

Individuals in the severe and profound categories need extensive training in self-care skills as well as some form of custodial supervision. In the trainable MR category, school programs frequently focus on developing self-care skills, language usage, independent living, perceptual motor abilities, and vocational skills. Those who are classified as educable MR may show a much slower rate of progress than nondisabled students in academic subjects, such as reading and math, and may have a final level of academic achievement between the second and sixth grades (Gage & Berliner, 1991).

There is an increasing tendency to drop these distinctions in favor of a generic retardation or cognitive disabilities level. The American Association on Mental Retardation (AAMR) defines retardation as:

> Mental retardation is defined as a substantial limitation in intellectual functioning (IQ 70 or below), significant limitations in two, or more, adaptive skill areas such as communication, self-care, home living, social skills, community use, self-direction, health and safety, functional academics, leisure, and work. The age of onset must occur at or before the age of 18. (AAMR, 1992, p. 1)

The measurement of deficits in adaptive behavior is subjective and depends on both the standards of the individuals making the judgment and the environment to which the student is expected to adapt (Ysseldyke & Algozzine, 1990). The AAMR definition provides a framework for the determination of the individual's functioning in a variety of environments.

Serious Emotional Disturbance

The conceptual definition of serious emotional disturbance presented in the federal regulations is:

"Serious emotional disturbance" is defined as follows:

1. The term means a condition exhibiting one or more of the following characteristics over a long period of time and to a marked degree, which adversely affects educational performance:
   (A) An inability to learn which cannot be explained by intellectual, sensory, or health factors;
   (B) An inability to build or maintain satisfactory interpersonal relationships with peers and teachers;
   (C) Inappropriate types of behavior or feelings under normal circumstances;
   (D) A general pervasive mood of unhappiness or depression; or
   (E) A tendency to develop physical symptoms or fears associated with personal or school problems.
2. The term includes children who are schizophrenic. The term does not include children who are socially maladjusted, unless it is determined that they are seriously emotionally disturbed. (34 Code of Federal Regulations 300.5 (a))

Gage and Berliner (1991) note that although the federal legislation uses the term *serious emotional disturbance,* educators tend to use the term *behavior disorders* so as to focus on the behavior that can be changed. Other educators prefer the term *students with challenging behaviors.* Operational definitions of behavior or emotional disorders may use psychological tests such as the Rorschach Ink Blot, Minnesota Multiphasic Personality Inventory, or the Vineland Social Maturity Scale, or clinical interviews administered by trained specialists, and supplemented by careful observations of the challenging behavior and the conditions under which it occurs.

Multiple Disabilities

A conceptual definition of multiple disabilities provided in the federal regulations states:

"Multiple disabilities" means concomitant impairments (such as mental retardation-blind, mental retardation-orthopedic impairments, etc.) the combination of which causes such severe educational problems that a child cannot be accommodated in special education programs solely for one of the impairments. The term does not include deaf-blindness. (34 Code of Federal Regulation 300.5 (a))

The heterogeneity of students who fit under this definition of multiple disabilities makes it especially important for researchers to describe the precise operational definition that is used. Constructing definitions or descriptions is difficult because the types and severity of the disabling conditions must be specified. Gee, Graham, Goetz, Oshima, and Yoshioka (1991) provided the following information about a student with multiple disabilities: blind (no light perception); physical disabilities and point of motor control (severe contractures and profound involvement of all four limbs; control over his head turn to the right [1 inch] when his head is supported; minimal control over his right arm movement away from his body (when assisted to bring his arm down to rest on his wheel chair tray); profound intellectual disability; and complex health care needs (severe seizure disorder, complex neurological and biobehavioral state changes, digestive/nutritional difficulties).

Hearing Impairments

The conceptual definition of hearing impairments provided in the federal regulations states:

"Hearing impairments" means either 1) a hearing impairment which is so severe that the child is impaired in processing linguistic information through hearing, with or without amplification (and would be considered to be deafness), and which adversely affects educational performance; or 2) a hearing impairment, whether permanent or fluctuating (which would not be considered to be deafness), and which adversely affects a child's educational performance. (34 Code of Federal Regulations 300.5(a))

In actuality, hearing disabilities range from total deafness to mild losses. Many operational definitions of hard of hearing and deafness have been developed (Bennett & Ragosta, 1988). Definitions of hearing loss are based on the two qualities of sound: loudness and pitch (Meadow, 1980). Loudness is measured in decibels (dB) from 0 for the softest sound to 120 for extremely loud sounds. Conversation is generally in the 60-70 dB range. Pitch, or frequency of sounds, is measured by hertz (Hz) or cycles per second. The frequencies that are most important for understanding speech are in the range of 500, 1,000, and 2,000 Hz. Paul and Quigley (1990, p. 41) provided the following operational definition of hearing loss based on results from the better unaided ear averaged across the speech frequencies, according to the International Standards Organization:

Degree of Impairment	Description
up to 26 decibels	Normal
27 to 40 decibels	Slight
41 to 55 decibels	Mild
56 to 70 decibels	Moderate
71 to 90 decibels	Severe
91+ decibels	Profound

Individuals in the slight, mild, and moderate categories are considered to be hard-of-hearing. Those in the severe and profound categories are considered to be deaf.

Certain general characteristics of deaf populations that have been reported have implications for conducting research. For example, students with mild losses rely mostly on speech when communicating with teachers and parents, and 85% have intelligible speech (Karchmer, Milone, & Wolk, 1979). Those with profound losses rely on manual communication, and only about 25% have intelligible speech. The students with severe losses fall between those with mild and profound losses. The median performance of hearing impaired 18-year-olds on reading comprehension ranged from third- to fourth-grade level on standard test norms (Trybus & Karchmer, 1977). (Note: Deaf children who are born to hearing parents often experience a delay in acquiring language, which affects their later abilities to learn to read. Academic performance is generally higher for students whose parents are deaf and who use American Sign Language from birth.)

Orthopedic Impairments

A conceptual definition of orthopedic impairments provided in the federal regulations states:

> "Orthopedic impairments" means a severe orthopedic impairment which adversely affects a child's educational performance. The term includes impairments caused by congenital anomaly (e.g., clubfoot, absence of some member, etc.), impairments caused by disease (e.g., poliomyelitis, bone tuberculosis, etc.), and impairments from other causes (e.g., cerebral

palsy, amputations, and fractures or burns which cause contractures). (34 Code of Federal Regulations 300.5 (a))

The category of orthopedic impairments includes a wide variety of impairments, some so mild as to be of no concern to the researcher. Some would require modification of the physical environment or additional means of communication or aids to instruction or locomotion. All would require a careful description of the subjects' characteristics. Bennett and Ragosta (1988) provide a detailed explanation of the characteristics usually associated with cerebral palsy, poliomyelitis, muscular dystrophy, multiple sclerosis, and impairments caused by physical injury (e.g., amputation of limb, or injury to spinal cord). For example, they describe characteristics associated with multiple sclerosis that would be of concern to the researcher, such as impaired sensation, lack of coordination, double vision, slurred speech, memory loss, spasticity or paralysis of extremities. The disease is progressive and unpredictable, and therefore, it would be important to clearly explain the status of the subjects in the study.

Other Health Impairments

The conceptual definition for other health impairments is presented in the federal regulations as follows:

"Other health impairments" means having limited strength, vitality or alertness, due to chronic or acute health problems such as a heart condition, tuberculosis, rheumatic fever, nephritis, asthma, sickle cell anemia, hemophilia, epilepsy, lead poisoning, leukemia, or diabetes, which adversely affects a child's educational performance. (34 Code of Federal Regulations 300.5(a))

This category also includes a wide variety of impairments, some of which would be of no concern to researchers. However, the researcher should be aware of the traditional classifications of such diseases as epilepsy (see Hallahan & Kauffman, 1978). While many diseases can be controlled with medication, the effects of medication on the subject's ability to participate in research must be considered. For example, medication for epilepsy can affect coordination, vision, attention, and memory.

Two emerging categories of children in need of special education include those with attention deficit hyperactivity (ADHD) or attention deficit disorder (ADD). Children with ADHD are hyperactive or disruptive and have trouble paying attention. The problem appears to be an inability to process information quickly enough when presented with too much information. As a result the child will tune out almost immediately and become either hyperactive (ADHD) or passive and lethargic (ADD).

During the 1990 reauthorization hearings of the IDEA, Congress rejected the inclusion of ADD and ADHD as separate categories in the legislation, because they took the position that children with these disabilities could meet the eligibility criteria for services in the current categories (Davila, Williams, & MacDonald, 1991). They stated:

> [C]hildren with ADD, where the ADD is a chronic or acute health problem resulting in limited alertness, may be considered disabled under Part B solely on the basis of this disorder within the "other health impaired" category in situations where special education and related services are needed because of the ADD. (p. 3) [Note: They used ADD as including ADD and ADHD.]

They further explained that children with ADD are also eligible for services if the children satisfy the criteria applicable to other disability categories, such as specific learning disability or serious emotionally disturbed.

A special issue of *Exceptional Children* addressed the issues surrounding attention deficit disorders (Hocutt, McKinney, & Montague, 1993). Readers who are interested in conducting research with this population are referred specifically to McBurnett, Lahey, and Pfiffner's (1993) article in that special issue, in which they summarized the results of the field trials for the forthcoming fourth edition of the American Psychiatric Association's *Diagnostic and Statistical Manual for Mental Disorders* regarding attention deficit disorders, and provided methods of operationalizing the concepts by measures of academic productivity and accuracy.

Visual Impairments

The federal regulations provide the following conceptual definition of visual impairments:

> "Visual impairments" means a visual impairment which, even with correction, adversely affects a child's educational performance. The term

includes both partially seeing and blind children. (34 Code of Federal Regulations 300.5 (a))

Visual impairments cover a wide range, from those with no vision whatsoever to those who can have 20/20 vision with corrective lenses. According to the National Society for the Prevention of Blindness (Reynolds & Birch, 1977, p. 605), partially sighted is defined as visual acuity in the better eye, with corrective lenses, that falls between 20/70 and 20/200. Legal blindness is defined as central visual acuity of 20/200 or less in the better eye with corrective lenses, or visual acuity greater than 20/200 if there is a restricted visual field subtending an angle no greater than 20 degrees. A more important distinction is based on the functional abilities of visually impaired individuals (Bennett & Ragosta, 1988). Most partially sighted and many legally blind individuals differ from totally blind individuals because they can use vision for participating in research, for example, reading large-type materials, holding pages close, and using magnification devices. Totally blind individuals depend on their tactual or auditory senses, thus using readers, Braille books, audio tapes, raised-line drawings, three-dimensional models, talking calculators, or Braille computers.

Deaf-Blindness

The conceptual definition of deaf-blindness provided in the federal regulations states:

> "Deaf-blindness" means concomitant hearing and visual impairments, the combination of which causes such severe communication and other developmental and educational problems that a child with deaf-blindness cannot be accommodated in special education programs solely for deaf or blind children. (34 Code of Federal Regulations 300.5 (a))

An operational definition of persons with deaf-blindness would combine the measurement of deafness described with the measurement of blindness discussed in the section on visual impairments. Students categorized as deaf-blind must also be described in terms of the presence of other disabling conditions. Researchers interested in working with the deaf-blind population should be aware that this group is also quite heterogeneous. Heterogeneity can be introduced through a number of variables, such as (1) variation in the range of hearing and vision loss, (2) presence of additional disabilities (it is estimated that about 60% of students with dual-sensory impairments also are severely to profoundly retarded [Paul & Quigley, 1990]), or (3) cause of the disabilities (e.g., Usher's syndrome involves progressive sensory impairment).

The Annual Survey of Hearing Impaired Children and Youth revealed that about 2% of the hearing impaired sample are legally blind, and another 4% have uncorrected visual problems (Wolff & Harkins, 1986). The high incidence of deaf-blindness and additional disabling conditions has led to the placement of many students in programs for multiple disabilities, rather than in programs that specialize in deaf-blindness (Paul & Quigley, 1990). Implications for researchers include: (1) care must be taken in reporting the characteristics of this heterogeneous group, and (2) access to subjects may be through programs for students with multiple disabilities, rather than deaf-blindness programs.

In one study that included a person with deaf-blindness, the authors described him as follows: some light perception in the left eye; functional hearing loss; physical disabilities and point of motor control (profound involvement in all four limbs, control over his right hand movement over and to the right, control of head turning when his head is down, holds head up for 5 seconds); profound intellectual disability; and complex health care needs (gastrointestinal degenerative disorder, severe seizure disorder) (Gee et al., 1991).

Autism

The federal regulations conceptual definition of autism is as follows:

"Autism" means a developmental disability significantly affecting verbal and non-verbal communication and social interaction, generally evident before age three, that adversely affects educational performance. Characteristics of autism include irregularities and impairments in communication, engagement in repetitive activities and stereotyped movements, resistance to environmental change or change in daily routines, and unusual responses to sensory experiences. The term does not include children with characteristics of the disability serious emotional disturbance. (34 Code of Federal Regulations 300.5(a))

In one study, autism was operationally defined on the basis of a diagnosis from an outside agency and the confirmation of that diagnosis by an experienced clinical psychologist (Harris, Handleman, Gordon, Kristoff, & Fuentes, 1991). They also used the Childhood Autism Rating Scale to measure autistic behavior.

Traumatic Brain Injury

The federal regulations conceptually define traumatic brain injury as follows:

> "Traumatic brain injury" means an injury to the brain caused by an external physical force or by an internal occurrence such as stroke or aneurysm, resulting in total or partial functional disability or psychosocial maladjustment that adversely affects educational performance. The term includes open or closed head injuries resulting in mild, moderate, or severe impairments in one or more areas, including cognition; language; memory; attention; reasoning; abstract thinking; judgment; problem-solving; sensory, perceptual and motor abilities; psychosocial behavior; physical functions; information processing; and speech. The term does not include brain injuries that are congenital or degenerative, or brain injuries induced by birth trauma. (34 Code of Federal Regulations 300.5(a))

Towne and Entwisle (1993) operationally defined traumatic brain injury by describing the amount of time that had passed since the injury in months, the duration of the coma following injury, the duration of post-traumatic amnesia, and the level of cognitive functioning as measured by the Level of Cognitive Functioning Scale (Hagen, Malkmus, Durham, & Bowman, 1979). Russell (1993) recommended inclusion of similar types of information in her paper on educational consideration in traumatic brain injury.

Infants and Toddlers With Disabilities

The federal regulations have defined a generic category called "infants and toddlers with disabilities" to cover the special education population for individuals from birth through age 2 who need early intervention services. The federal definition of this group states that the children:

1. Are experiencing developmental delays, as measured by appropriate diagnostic instruments and procedures in one or more of the following areas:
    (i) Cognitive development;
    (ii) Physical development, including vision and hearing;
    (iii) Language and speech development;
    (iv) Psychosocial development; or

(v) Self-help skills.

2. Have a diagnosed physical or mental condition that has a high probability of resulting in developmental delay.

(i) The term may also include, at a State's discretion, children from birth through age two who are at risk of having substantial developmental delays if early intervention services are not provided. (34 Code of Federal Regulations 303.16)

Interventions with infants and toddlers typically involve both the child and the family, and can be both center- and home-based.

Developmental Delay and At Risk

Two terms in the infants and toddler legislation (i.e., developmentally delayed and at risk) require definition. The federal government asked that states develop a definition for developmental delay that:

1. Specify that a child may be determined to be *eligible* if the child has a delay ... in one or more of the following developmental areas: cognitive development, physical development, including vision and hearing; language and speech development; psychosocial development; or self-help skills;

2. Designate the levels of functioning, or other criteria, that will be used in determining a child's eligibility as a result of developmental delay; and

3. Describe the procedures the State will use to determine the existence of a developmental delay in each developmental area included in paragraph 1 of this section. (34 Code of Federal Regulations 303.300)

Conditions that are associated with developmental delay include Down syndrome and other chromosomal abnormalities; sensory impairments including vision and hearing; inborn errors of metabolism; microcephaly; severe attachment disorders, including failure to thrive; seizure disorders; and fetal alcohol syndrome.

In November 1990, 23 states included children at risk in their definition of the developmentally delayed infants and toddlers (U.S. Department of Education, 1991). The states included children who were at risk due to either environmental factors or biological factors or both. The federal regulations advise states that in defining the at-risk population,

[s]tates may include well-known biological and other factors that can be identified during the neonatal period, and that place infants "at risk" for developmental delay. Commonly cited factors relating to infants include low birth weight, respiratory distress as a newborn, lack of oxygen, brain hemorrhage, and infection. It should be noted that these factors do not predict the presence of a barrier to development, but they may indicate children who are at higher risk of developmental delay than children without these problems. (34 Code of Federal Regulations Ch. III (7-1-90 Edition) 303.16, Note 2, p. 113)

Researchers should explain the meaning of developmental delay and at risk following the parameters set forth in the federal regulations, that is, specifying the area(s) of developmental delay, the level of functioning, and criteria and procedures that were used to determine the child's status. For example, one study included 124 children, ages 3-6 years, with mild and moderate disabilities (Cole, Mills, Dale, & Jenkins, 1991). The researchers clarified the meaning of developmentally delayed with the following information:

includes children with deficits of at least 1.5 standard deviations below the mean in two or more of the areas of cognitive, language, social, gross motor, and fine motor development, or 2 standard deviations below the mean in any one area. Regarding specific diagnostic categories, approximately 80% of the subjects were delayed in language, 50% were cognitively delayed, 65% exhibited fine motor deficits, 60% demonstrated delays in gross motor deficits, and 60% exhibited social-emotional delays. (p. 37)

DESIGNING AND SELECTING SAMPLES

Rarely is it possible or even necessary to collect data on all the individuals in a group (e.g., there are more than 2 million students who are considered to be learning disabled). The target population is defined as all the members of a group of people to whom we wish to generalize the results of our research. For example, the target population in the study of the employment experiences of females with disabilities (as compared to males) is the U.S. population of students in special education in the 1985-1986 school year who were in grades 7 through 12 or at least 13 years old (Wagner, 1992). Those individuals from whom data are actually collected are called a sample. The sample Wagner used included more than 8,000 youths, ages 13 to 21, and special education students in secondary schools in the 1985-1986 school year.

A researcher has three main options for the selection of the sample: *probability-based sampling, purposeful sampling,* or *volunteer sampling.* Each of these options will be discussed briefly below. For more detailed explanations, the reader is referred to Borg and Gall (1989), Henry (1990), Krathwohl (1993), Lipsey (1990), or Stainback and Stainback (1988).

Probability-Based Sampling

Simple Random Sampling. Simple random sampling means that each individual in the defined population has an equal and independent chance of being selected as a member of the sample. Independent means that the selection of one individual does not affect the selection of anyone else. Simple random sampling techniques yield research data that can be generalized to a larger population, within margins of error that can be determined statistically, and it allows the use of inferential statistics (explained in Chapter 7) for group comparisons. Simple random samples can be generated in a number of ways, for example, by computer generation of random numbers; putting all the names of the individuals in the population into a hat and drawing them out "at random"; or using a table of random numbers, randomly selecting a row or column in the table, and then taking all the numbers in that row or column until enough subjects have been selected.

Systematic Sampling. This technique can be used if all the names of the defined population are on a list which is not in some systematic order that would create a bias in the sample. It involves choosing every *n*th name from the list. For example, if you need to select 100 subjects from a list of 1,000 individuals, divide the needed sample size by the number of individuals on the list (1,000/100 = 10). Then pick a random number less than 10 as a place to start on the list and choose every 10th name.

Stratified Sampling. In many situations, the researcher will want to do subgroup analyses with the data (e.g., comparing hard of hearing students with deaf students, or African-Americans with Caucasians). In these circumstances, stratified sampling is needed in order to have proportionate samples for the subgroup analyses. The desired strata (i.e., categories to be used for comparison) are defined, and individuals are randomly sampled within those strata (Henry, 1990; Lipsey, 1990).

This is the type of sampling that Wagner (1992) used to study gender differences. The list of students in the target population was stratified into three age groups (13 to 15, 16 to 18, over 18) for each of the federal special education disability categories, and youths were randomly selected from each age/disability group so that approximately 800 to 1,000 students were selected in each disability category (with the exception of deaf-blind, for which fewer than 100 students were served in the districts and schools included in the sample). If the researcher expects to have small samples in subgroups, Lipsey (1990) explains how to oversample certain groups and adjust for small cell sizes.

Cluster Sampling. The researcher may find it easier to get a list of all the schools with more than 20 visually impaired students than to get a list of all visually impaired students. Therefore, the researcher can start with a list of the schools and randomly select schools from the list. Then, data can be collected from all individuals at those schools, or a random sample of the students within those schools can be obtained for multistage cluster sampling.

Purposeful Sampling

Patton (1990) identified the following types of purposeful sampling:

- *Sampling extreme or deviant cases.* Particularly unusual cases are selected in order to shed light on a specific problem, for example, the most and least successful students in the program.
- *Sampling typical cases.* Individuals are chosen because they represent typical cases in a program (i.e., not extreme or deviant cases).
- *Maximum variation sampling.* Cases are selected that represent a range on some dimension, for example, students who are mainstreamed for varying amounts of time during the school day.
- *Sampling critical cases.* Cases are selected that are particularly important, based on some criteria of special significance to the researcher or the intended user of the research data, for example, including all students who had speech therapy prior to starting elementary school.
- *Sampling politically important or sensitive cases.* This is a variation of the critical cases sampling strategy in which the researcher samples (or avoids sampling) politically important or sensitive cases, for example, a board member's child.
- *Convenience sampling.* The researcher takes the sample that is easiest to come by.

In qualitative research, sampling is relatively flexible, often starting with a procedure referred to as *snowballing*, that is, using initially selected participants to recommend other participants (Stainback & Stainback, 1988). The researcher then moves on to purposeful sampling, in which participants are included according to relevant criteria determined by the researcher, based on an analysis of the data being collected and the emerging research questions. Many researchers who write from the reform ideology reject the term *subject* as dehumanizing (Reinharz, 1992). They prefer to use a term such as *participant*, thus recognizing the active exchange of information that occurs between the researcher and those who are asked to provide information in the study.

Volunteer Samples

For practical, ethical, and legal reasons, a researcher may not be able to use either random or purposeful sampling. Because consent forms must be signed in most research studies with human subjects, nearly all educational research must be conducted with volunteer samples. Research on volunteer samples indicates that they tend to be better educated, from higher social-class status, and more intelligent (Borg & Gall, 1989). Therefore, research conducted with volunteer subjects generally tends to yield an optimistic picture of a treatment's effects.

SPECIAL EDUCATION
SAMPLING ISSUES

The heterogeneity, as well as the inconsistency in classification, of special education groups was mentioned in the section on definition of populations. In addition to those problems, other issues related to sampling are specific to research in special education.

Unique Factors Specific to
Special Education Populations

For each special education group, several variables are uniquely associated with an accurate depiction of the nature of the individuals selected. For example, Mertens (1990b, 1991b) identified the following unique variables associated with deaf populations:

1. Family background characteristics: hearing status of parents and communication mode used in the home.
2. Student background characteristics: age at which loss occurred, degree and cause of loss, communication skills, degree of loss, hearing aid usage, presence of additional disabilities, and intelligibility of speech.
3. School or school district conditions: size of deaf student enrollment, support services, expenditures.
4. Within-school conditions: deaf student-teacher ratio.
5. Instructional personnel characteristics: signing ability, training and experience working with deaf students.
6. Student attitudes: impulsivity, internal/external control.
7. Student placement: residential, mainstreamed, self-contained classrooms.
8. Instructional personnel, including teachers and interpreters: communication mode used in the classroom/home.

Given the heterogeneity found within the special education populations, researchers must include an explanation of the characteristics that are unique to that population.

Practical Considerations

The number and distribution of special education students impacts the sample design and size (Wang, Reynolds, & Walberg, 1990). For example, in Florida, almost all of the districts with full-time programs for students with visual impairments have fewer than 20 students in the entire district. With potential subjects scattered among many schools, the difficulty of identifying a sample and the variability of contextual factors increases. Particularly with low-incidence populations, this increases the expense of travel and complicates obtaining the necessary informed consents.

The changing patterns in educational settings are exemplified by the area of deafness, where enrollment in residential schools decreased between 1978 and 1988 by 38%, with fewer than 10,000 of the 46,000 deaf students enrolled in residential schools (Schildroth, 1989). During that 10-year period, the number of individual schools serving deaf students increased substantially, growing from 4,789 in 1978 to 8,310 in 1988. Approximately half (4,096 of the 8,310) of the programs had only one deaf student enrolled in 1988.

Comparison Group

In many research designs, the students' performance or characteristics are compared with those of another sample that varies on some specified characteristic (the comparison group). DeStefano and Wagner (1991) discussed options and problems associated with selecting an appropriate comparison group. They described four common comparison groups:

The general population can be used as a comparison. Often extant data are available for such a comparison from such data bases as High School and Beyond and National Longitudinal Survey of Youth. But students with disabilities differ from nondisabled peers in important ways. As a part of the National Longitudinal Transition Study, Marder and Cox (1990) reported that the disabled population contained more males, blacks, urban dwellers, people with lower incomes (<$25,000), household heads without high school diplomas, and single-parent households. Also, other mediating factors differentiate the general education population from the disabled population, such as participation in special school programs, decreased options for interaction with nondisabled peers, and social stigma.

Comparisons across disability categories is an option. It is important to disaggregate data by disability groups because of the heterogeneity that has been discussed previously. There is also heterogeneity within categories that must be addressed, such as variations in IQ levels in the Learning Disabled category.

Cross-unit comparisons involve the comparison of students with disabilities in one school or school district with students in another school or school district. In such comparisons, the researcher must be sensitive to demographic differences and differences in the educational philosophies, policies, and practices.

Longitudinal studies allow comparison with one group at two or more points in time. The researcher must again be sensitive to historical influences, such as changes in demographic conditions, policy (e.g., changes in graduation requirements), or economic conditions in the community.

Sample Size

Insufficient sample size can be a problem because of the practical considerations discussed previously, but also because of the need to disaggregate the data or because of attrition (DeStefano & Wagner,

1991). When it is necessary to disaggregate the sample by disability areas, race, gender, or other variables, the sample cell sizes may become too small for meaningful interpretation. For example, in a study of reclassification trends in special education, the researchers were interested in the impact of a change in service district on the reclassification rate (Mertens, Harper, Haigh, & Hayden, 1992). However, only 4% of the sample changed service districts during the 3-year period of the study. Therefore, sample sizes disaggregated by disability condition and age would have been too small to make meaningful interpretations. Henry (1990) describes strategies for weighting in subpopulation analyses, and Lipsey (1990) describes ways to design research that will be sufficiently sensitive to detect the intended effects.

Attrition is a second reason for small sample sizes (DeStefano & Wagner, 1991). In the National Longitudinal Transition Study, researchers experienced a 2% per year loss for youths who were in the first wave of the survey in 1987, with higher attrition rates for older youths and those who were no longer in secondary school. They recommended that the initial sample size be increased by an appropriate percentage so that the desired sample size would still be available at the end of the study.

Sampling Error and Sampling Bias

Sampling error is the difference between characteristics of the sample and the population, and can be estimated with random samples (DeStefano & Wagner, 1991). The sampling error is a function of sample size; smaller samples have larger errors associated with them. When probability sampling is used, the researcher should report estimates of sampling error (e.g., see Sudman, 1976). *Sampling bias* affects the generalizability of the study. The researcher must explore potential bias and present potential bias to the reader. To assess bias, the researcher must determine the comparability of the population that the sample purports to represent and the sample of subjects for which data are available.

Henry (1990) identified a number of factors that affect bias. Two of these include response rate and the extent to which students who were included differ from those the sample is purported to represent. Sample bias increases as response rate decreases, because of the heterogeneity of a small sample. Therefore, with survey research in particular, followup of nonrespondents and comparison of nonrespondents with respondents is essential.

GENERALIZABILITY,
EXTERNAL VALIDITY, AND TRANSFERABILITY

In the positivist paradigm, external validity is the extent to which the findings of a study can be applied to people and settings outside the research study (Borg & Gall, 1989). Population validity is one source of external validity that concerns the extent to which the results of an experiment can be generalized from the specific sample that was studied to a larger group of subjects. In the empiricist tradition, the question is asked: To what extent can I generalize from the study sample to a defined population?

In the constructivist paradigm, Guba and Lincoln (1989) suggest that the criterion of transferability should be used to answer the question: How can we determine the degree to which the findings of a particular inquiry may have applicability in other contexts or with other respondents? The two strategies they suggest for dealing with this issue are thick description and use of purposeful sampling. Thick description means that the narrative is developed in such a way that judgments about the degree of fit or similarity may be made by others who may wish to apply all or part of the findings elsewhere. Purposeful sampling was previously discussed in the section on designing and selecting samples.

ETHICS AND CONFIDENTIALITY

Researchers in special education must follow appropriate ethical principles to ensure that the rights of human subjects are protected, such as those developed by the American Psychological Association for conducting research with human subjects (Committee on Scientific and Professional Ethics and Conduct, 1981). Sieber (1992) offered a logical ethical framework to guide researchers and those responsible for the ethical review of research, based on the federal regulations that require protection of human subjects. This includes the use of an Institutional Review Board to safeguard the subjects' rights and to ensure that proper procedures are followed with reference to subjects' consent to participate in research.

Special education has had a strong ethical component since its inception because it developed largely from a commitment to the ethical requirement that all individuals be provided with access to a decent public education, regardless of how they might differ from the general population with respect to various skills, abilities, and powers that affect school performance (Howe & Miramontes, 1991). The Council for Exceptional Children (CEC) developed a formal ethical code that addressed the specific ethics of conducting research with special education populations (Council for Exceptional Children, 1983). CEC's code of ethics states that special education professionals are required to protect the rights and welfare of subjects, interpret and publish research results with accuracy and a high quality of scholarship, support a cessation of the use of any research procedure that may result in undesirable consequences for the participants, and exercise all possible precautions to prevent misapplication or misuse of a research effort. Special education researchers, like practitioners, must be alert to the implicit value commitments and consequences that attend categorizing individuals as learning disabled, mentally retarded, and so on. The researcher must grapple with the problem of trying to balance general principles that apply to special education populations with the values and interests that characterize individual cases.

Guidelines for research in educational programs have been published within several disability areas. For example, the Conference of Executives of American Schools for the Deaf published guidelines for research in educational programs for the deaf (1979). In addition to requiring adherence to the federal regulations, the review board is encouraged to consider whether the researcher demonstrates an adequate understanding of deafness and its consequences, and the multivariate nature of the educational process, to enable the research to produce meaningful findings. Researchers in other disability areas should be aware of parallel guidelines in those areas.

The view of ethics as written about by feminists and minorities has parallel (though not exact) applicability to persons with disabilities (Mertens, 1993b). For example, in Cook and Fonow's (1990) discussion of the feminist perspective of ethics in research, they note the use of language as a means of subordination, such as the use of masculine pronouns, application of offensive adjectives to women's experiences, and the subsumption of women under male categories. Parallels exist in the writings of minorities about race research, such as defining single motherhood as a moral/social problem (e.g., broken home) when it applies to minority women, but as an alternative family structure when it applies to white women. Stanfield (1993) notes that how elites talk and write has a profound role in reproducing the racial order of things. Social science discourse involves an elite way of talking and writing that in race-centered societies creates a public image of the dominant and of the oppressed that appears to be objective and value-free. Oppressive use of language persists in the identification of persons with disabilities. Even the word *disability* is negative, defined in terms of what can't be done. In the area of deafness, deaf people prefer to be thought of as a cultural group that uses visual-gestural communication, not as a group who *can't* hear.

QUESTIONS FOR CRITICALLY ANALYZING SAMPLE DESIGN AND IMPLEMENTATION

1. What is the population of interest? How was the sample chosen? Probability? Purposeful? Volunteer?
2. What are the characteristics of the sample? To whom can you generalize the results? Is adequate information given about the characteristics of the sample?
3. How large is the population? How large is the sample? What is the effect of the sample size on the interpretation of the results?
4. Is the sample selected related to the target population?
5. Who dropped out during the research? Were they different from those who completed the study?
6. In qualitative research, was thick description used in the description of the sample?
7. In qualitative research, what is the effect of using purposeful sampling on the transferability to other situations?
8. Are female subjects excluded, even when the research question affects both sexes? Are male subjects excluded, even when the research affects both sexes?
9. Does the researcher report the sample composition by gender and other background characteristics, such as race/ethnicity and class?

QUESTIONS AND ACTIVITIES FOR DISCUSSION AND APPLICATION

1. Why is it important for the researcher to provide specific explanations of the methods used to identify and select the sample?
2. Where do you stand on the "labeling" controversy? Should labels be abandoned as misleading, or retained as functional?

3. What is the difference between a conceptual and an operational definition? Give an example of each.

4. Choose one conceptual definition of a disability area. Brainstorm as many ways as you can to operationally define that area. What are the strengths and weaknesses of the different operational definitions you generated?

5. What are the differences between the three types of sampling strategies: probability-based, purposeful, and volunteer/convenience? Describe a situation in which you might use each type of sampling strategy. What are the advantages and disadvantages of each?

6. How do factors that are unique to each disability area influence sampling?

7. What problems are encountered in trying to select an appropriate comparison group?

8. What do generalizability and external validity mean? How can they be enhanced in a research study?

9. Using the questions for critical analysis (1 through 5, 8, and 9), critique the following description of a sample and suggest alternatives to improve the study:

In a study of intellectual functioning of children with autism, children from two classes in a developmental disabilities center participated (Harris et al., 1991). One class (the segregated class) served only children with autism, while the other was an integrated class that includes normally developing children. Because they did not have enough peers from the integrated class to provide a comparison group, they used an additional four children from a university day-care facility. The sample for the study of intellectual functioning included nine children with autism and nine normally developing children. There was one girl in each group.

10. Using the questions for critical analysis (1 through 9), critique the following description of a sample and suggest alternatives to improve the study:

Sue, Andrew, and John attended an early intervention preschool for hearing-impaired children that focused on supporting the children's acquisition of language, be it spoken or signed, as a prerequisite to literacy learning. The preschool was divided into three levels, Preschool I, Preschool II, and Kindergarten, and children were placed according to age and mode of communication, that is, either oral/aural English or total communication. Sue (age 3.11), Andrew (age 5.0), and John (age 5.10) were chosen to participate as case studies because they each had profound hearing losses, they had hearing parents, there was some difference in their socio-economic status, and their verbal language worlds reflected the multiplicity, diversity, and variability typically experienced by profoundly deaf children (Williams, Kantor, & Pinnell, 1992, p. 5).

6

Information Collection

Did students with mental retardation increase their ability to use socially acceptable interaction skills as a result of the new intervention? Were they able to effectively use the skills in the classroom? Did the learning transfer to other settings, including the home? What was the cost of the intervention? Did the experimenters use learning strategies appropriate for learners with mental retardation? Did the students have the necessary entry level skills to be able to benefit from the social skills training?

The common theme to all of these questions is the need for information. We acquire information about people, products, programs, organizations, and environments through the process of data collection in order to answer research questions and defend conclusions and recommendations, based on the findings from the research. The objectives of this chapter are to explore the issues and processes for data collection from persons with disabilities.

In This Chapter

- The purpose of information collection in relation to the needs of the research is presented.
- Accommodations necessary for collection of data from persons with disabilities are discussed.
- The basic types of information sources available to the researcher are set forth.
- Criteria for judging the technical adequacy of data collection instruments are described.
- Suggestions for selecting and using data collection instruments are discussed.
- Questions for critically analyzing information collection in research are provided.

THE PURPOSE OF INFORMATION COLLECTION

The purpose of information collection is to learn something about people or things. The focus is on a particular attribute or quality of the person or thing being measured. For example, MacMillan, Widaman, Balow, Hemsley, and Little (1992) were interested in how students with learning disabilities felt about school. Thus, the attribute that they were measuring was attitude toward school.

Researchers face two challenges when developing the information collection strategies for the proposed research: First, the attribute(s) to be measured must be identified; and second, a decision must be made about how to measure the attribute(s). The process of determining how to measure the attribute is referred to as *operationalizing*. For example, MacMillan et al. (1992) operationalized the concept of attitudes toward school by selecting the *Survey of School Attitudes* (SSA) (Hogan, 1975) as their dependent measure.

As noted in Chapter 2, the research questions or hypotheses guide the researchers' response to these two challenges. A major resource is the literature review, but it is also suggested that the researcher discuss the proposed research with other professionals interested in the same research topic. The purpose is to identify what others have considered relative to the targeted attributes and their measurement. Data collection from persons with disabilities often requires modifications in strategies and materials from those described for the nondisabled populations.

TYPES OF ACCOMMODATIONS

Thurlow, Ysseldyke, and Silverstein (1993) summarized the current status regarding knowledge about accommodations in testing students with disabilities as follows: "There does not currently exist a set of guidelines about acceptable accommodations that is based on comprehensive, empirical research" (p. 3). Based on an extensive review of the literature, they identified the following accommodations that are used in testing persons with disabilities: Braille, audiocassette, large-print tests, oral reading of the text, large-type answer sheets, changing the test environment, flexible time arrangements (e.g., unlimited time or taking the test over several sessions to alleviate fatigue), signing instructions, and various assistive devices, such as Braillers, slate and stylus, magnifying glass, or tape recorder.

Although we do not have a comprehensive empirical base to help us understand the effect of these accommodations on test performance, the Educational Testing Service's research on the Graduate Record Examination did reveal various accommodations that were necessary for students of differential abilities (Bennett & Ragosta, 1988). For students with learning disabilities, poor reading skills might prevent accurate performance, because of a lack of understanding of the test instructions and problems presented in context (e.g., word problems in math). Therefore, they recommended the use of modifications to testing conditions, such as using cassette tapes. For deaf students, they recommended use of sign language for instructions, videotapes, and performance-based rather than language-based measurement of cognitive and spatial abilities. Bennett and Ragosta recognized that the level of visual ability would influence the need for test accommodations. For partially sighted subjects, large type, holding the page close, and use of magnification devices could be used. Subjects who are totally blind can augment their tactual or auditory senses by the use of readers, Braille books, audio tapes, raised-line drawings, three-dimensional models, talking calculators, and Braille computers. For subjects who are physically disabled, they recommended use of an amanuensis (person who records responses), and allowing extra time because of fatigue. The influence of these accommodations on the technical adequacy of the data collection instrument is explored in a later section of this chapter.

SOURCES OF INFORMATION

Hedrick, Bickman, and Rog (1993) identified two types of information sources available to researchers: primary and secondary. Primary information sources include people (program participants), observations of events (classroom instruction), physical documents (products/projects), and assessments (achievement tests). Secondary sources include administrative records (placement records), prior research studies (data collected by other researchers), national databases (the National Assessment of Educational Progress [NAEP]), and various forms of documentary evidence (evaluation reports).

Primary Information Sources

Collection of data from people can be accomplished through surveys and interviews. These two methods, along with observation, are discussed in Chapters 3 and 4; therefore, we will not discuss them further here. Physical documents were also discussed in Chapter 4, except for the concept of student portfolios, which is an emerging strategy for collecting data about student performance (U.S. Department of Education, 1993b). Portfolios are collections of student work representing a selection of performance, such as written assignments, videotapes, or solutions to math problems. In the state of Kentucky, 2% of its students with disabilities participate in an alternative portfolio assessment system instead of taking the state's minimum competency test (Thurlow et al., 1993). The U.S. Department of Education's newsletter *Consumer Guide* (1993c), and UCLA's Center for Research on Evaluation, Standards, and Student Testing's *CRESST Line* (1992-1993), provide resources and references for the use of student portfolios.

Tests. Tests are used extensively in research to collect information about student performance. To make the researcher's selection of the appropriate measurement device easier, it is helpful to categorize the numerous types of measures. Several classes of measurement devices are briefly reviewed below.

We begin with a comparison of *standardized* and *nonstandardized* tests. When compared to the nonstandardized test, the most distinguishing characteristic of the standardized test is its uniformity in directions for administering and scoring the instrument, as well as the developmental cycle that it goes through. The nonstandardized test is usually not developed through a rigorous process and has a limited purpose and application, such as the teacher-made test or that developed by a researcher for a specific study.

With standardized tests, there is a reference group of people, who participated in the standardization of the test, to which researchers can compare the performance of their subjects. This reference group is referred to as the *norm group*. Its raw scores on the test are compiled into norm tables, often in the form of percentile ranks, which furnish the percentage of students in the norm group who received the same score or lower. Researchers using the test can compare the performance of their subjects to the norm tables.

Researchers who choose to use standardized measures are faced with the challenge of locating an instrument that was developed with a norm group that matches the research sample. If the research sample is composed of students with learning disabilities, then the researcher would have to check the test manual to identify the characteristics of the norm group to determine if students with learning disabilities were in the norm group, and if there was a norm table specifically for this group. Unfortunately, tests that are standardized are usually globally referenced to the general population. Thus, most standardized tests do not contain information about the performance of persons with specific disabilities, and persons with more severe disabilities are most frequently omitted. This does not mean that the test could not be used in research directed at this population. Rather, it would be inappropriate to use the norms for interpretations or generalizations. As noted in Chapter 2, the researcher should review the literature to see how other researchers have dealt with this problem in using the proposed measurement device.

Several other classes of measurement devices can be identified, all of which can be standardized or nonstandardized. These include *individual* or *group* tests, where the former is administered to individuals and the latter is administered in a group setting. This distinction is important in special education because, for some attributes (e.g., intelligence), individual tests may be more appropriate than group tests (for some disability groups). There also are *speed* and *power* tests. Speed tests are made up of relatively simple items, but the administration requires very short response time for the test. On the other hand, power tests are composed of difficult items that are responded to in a more liberal time frame. This distinction is also important in special education, because students with certain disabilities may require additional time, and thus would be penalized on speed tests.

Norm referenced and *criterion or domain referenced* measurement devices represent other types of measurement. Most standardized achievement tests are norm referenced. The purpose of the norm referenced test is to enable the researcher to compare the performance of an individual to the performance of like individuals in a well-defined, previously tested group. On the other hand, the criterion referenced or domain referenced test addresses the content or domain of the attribute being measured. The intent is to identify how much of the attribute, as defined by the domain, has been acquired or learned, rather than comparing the performance to other subjects, as in the norm referenced test. The concept of criterion is applied when the researcher identifies a particular level of performance that subjects should reach as a result of being exposed to a particular intervention.

Three different types of assessment are emerging: performance assessment, curriculum-based assessment, and assessment using computers. According to Berk (1986), *performance assessment* is a process for collecting information through systematic observation in order to make decisions about an individual. The key concepts here are process and systematic observation. Performance assessment relies on the use of multiple types of assessments, not a single test or measurement device, and assessment occurs across time. Further, the primary vehicle for assessment is the direct observation of performance in the form of behavior and products.

Curriculum-based assessment is designed to collect information on the instructional needs of students through the continuous, direct observation of student performance (Fuchs & Deno, 1991). The assessment is keyed to the existing curriculum content and is based on enroute and terminal instructional objectives. The information collected reflects both the student's approach to the learning task and the products developed.

Both performance and curriculum-based assessment have been used in educational settings to produce information about individuals. The information typically generated is not used to make decisions about a program or group. Further, some who criticize the use of these approaches indicate that they are labor-intensive, prone to subjectivity, and, because of their link to a specific curriculum, have limited generalizability. More in-depth discussion of performance assessment can be found in Berk (1986), Finch (1991), Starlin (1992), and the Center for Research on Evaluation, Standards, and Student Testing's *CRESST Line* (1992-1993) and *Evaluation Comment* (1993). Additional information on curriculum-based assessment may be found in Bigge (1988), Fuchs and Deno (1991), and Fuchs and Fuchs (1986).

The Educational Testing Service is studying the use of *computers in testing* in terms of videodisc systems that display written text simultaneously with an insert of a person translating the text into sign language, voice synthesizers that simulate speech for individuals who are blind, and movement controls that allow a person with difficulty speaking and limited hand movement to both enter text and respond to text presented on the monitor (ETS, 1992). The National Center for Fair and Open Testing (FairTest, 1993) raised questions about the use of computers in testing with persons with disabilities, such as: Is there adequate evidence that scores of computerized and paper-and-pencil tests are equivalent? Will computerized tests constrain users because they cannot underline, scratch out eliminated choices, or scan materials in the same way they can with paper-and-pencil tests? Additional research is needed in this area in order to answer these questions.

Secondary Sources

Several of the secondary sources, such as administrative records and prior research studies, have been discussed in previous chapters. Researchers should be aware that there is a considerable information base available for special education research. For example, the federal government requires schools to collect and report data associated with the delivery of services to students with disabilities. These data include information not only on students served, but also on their placement and those who serve them. However, as Maruyama and Deno (1992) note, using extant data sets has its drawbacks. Often, the information is collected to inform policy, not theory development, and is collected at a level that does not allow disaggregation. Further, some national data bases actually exclude certain categories of persons. For example, NAEP excludes educable mentally retarded students and those with functional disabilities (unless they can respond to the tasks) (NASDE, 1988). The exclusion decision is the responsibility of the local school division. Thus, the researcher cannot be sure who is included in the data set.

Variations in the criteria for inclusion, and in the implementation of modifications to testing procedures, represent challenges for the use of existing data bases in special education research. The basis for inclusion of students with disabilities, and the types of acceptable modifications across states in minimum competency programs, is quite variable (McGrew, Thurlow, & Spiegel, 1993; Thurlow et al., 1993). In addition, McGrew et al. (1993) reported exclusion rates on the NAEP for students with disabilities that ranged from 33% to 87% across states. The variability in inclusion criteria and accommodations yields test results that are not easily interpretable across groups.

TECHNICAL ADEQUACY OF
DATA COLLECTION INSTRUMENTS

The degree of confidence the researcher and those who intend to use the research findings can place on the research depends in large part on the quality of the measurement procedures. The three methods typically employed to assess the quality of measurement in the positivist, quantitative tradition are reliability, validity, and objectivity. Parallel criteria for qualitative approaches have been discussed in Chapter 4.

Reliability

In order to be useful, measurement instruments must be consistent. When we measure a particular attribute, we are concerned about the accurate estimate of the target attribute. If you were to test your students' ability to solve word problems one day and, without additional instruction in math, give them the same test the next time they came to class, you would expect that their scores on the word problem test would be about the same. Ability to solve word problems, like most attributes, does not vary across time without some intervention. In the previous example, if your students' scores changed, then their performance must have been influenced by something other than their ability to solve math word problems. These other influences cause error; the extent to which measurement instruments are free from error indicates their reliability. The more reliable the measurement, the closer the researcher can arrive at a true estimate of the attribute addressed by the measure.

The purpose of measurement is to get an accurate or error-free estimate of a particular attribute. There are two types of error that can influence performance on a measurement instrument: *systematic* and *unsystematic*. Systematic errors inflate or deflate performance in a fixed way and thus do not affect a measure's reliability. In the above example, additional math instruction could be thought of as a systematic influence on performance. The effect of a systematic error on performance is constant and therefore can be predicted.

It is the unsystematic errors that concern researchers. These vary at random from situation to situation and therefore cannot be predicted. Unsystematic errors are produced by factors that fall into three categories: those within the person being measured, the conditions of the administration of the measurement, and changes in the measurement instrument or tasks.

Examples of factors within the individual that could randomly influence behavior are motivation and alertness. Students with attention deficit disorders might have difficulty maintaining concentration across a number of research tasks. Unsystematic changes (those that are not done for the students) in the administration that might influence performance include providing different instructions, changing the environment, or allowing more time. When the items on the instrument or the behaviors being sampled are changed, fluctuations in performance also may arise.

The reliability of a measurement instrument is typically established by comparing performance of the same individuals across time and is expressed in the form of a coefficient of correlation ranging from .00 to 1.00, with 1.00 indicating perfect reliability, which is rarely accomplished for any measure. The closer to 1.00, the more reliable the instrument. Most reliability coefficients range from .75 to .95. The important thing to remember is that anything less than 1.00 indicates the presence of error. The researcher's task is to identify the potential sources of such error and make them public.

How is reliability determined? There are several approaches that researchers can use to determine the reliability of a particular measurement device. The most common are described below. For a more thorough review the reader should consult a text on measurement, such as Ebel (1979), Mehrens and Lehmann (1984), or Thorndike and Hagen (1989).

Test-Retest. Test-retest reliability is established by administering the same test to the same individuals on two separate occasions. The second administration can occur either immediately or after a time lapse. Scores from both administrations are correlated to determine the consistency of response. One of the drawbacks of this approach is the potential for practice effect or remembering items across administrations of the test. For example, the test-retest reliability of the WISC Verbal scale for blind students was reported to be .91, which is generally comparable to those reported for the WISC standardization sample (Tillman, 1973).

Parallel Tests. If practice effects are a concern, then an equivalent (parallel) form of the test can be used in the second administration. Of course, the major concern with the parallel form's reliability check is the degree to which the two tests are equivalent. For example, Schunk and Rice (1992) studied the influence of comprehension strategies on reading achievement in remedial readers. Because they believed the passage familiarity might confound measurement of performance on the dependent variable in a posttest administration, they developed a parallel form that had a .87 correlation with the first form of the test.

Internal Consistency. For estimating internal stability or consistency, the researcher can either use a statistical method such as Cronbach's Coefficient Alpha or the Kuder-Richardson approaches (Borg & Gall, 1989), or the split-half method in which the two scores for the test are derived by summing the odd and then the even responses. The assumption here is that breaking the test according to odd and even items will result in two equivalent forms of the test. For example, in the MacMillan et al. (1992) investigation of attitudes toward school held by students with learning disabilities, the authors cited split-half and alpha reliability coefficients ranging from .77 to .99 on the *Survey of School Attitudes* (SSA) (Hogan, 1975) as evidence to support their selection.

Validity

In determining the appropriateness of a measure for a proposed research study, the researcher needs to be concerned with not only reliability but also validity. The conventional definition of the validity of a test is the extent to which it measures what it was constructed to measure. In practice, however, the validity of an instrument is assessed in relation to the extent to which evidence can be generated in support of the claim that the instrument measures attributes targeted in the proposed research.

An overarching concern in the study of validity is the extent to which the test measures the attributes it was intended to measure, and not bias due to gender, race/ethnicity, class, or disability. To be valid, testing must be nondiscriminatory; that is, tests and procedures used to evaluate a child's special needs must be free of bias based on gender, race, ethnicity, class, disability, or other cultural factors in both the way they are administered and the content of the items on the test. Suran and Rizzo (1983) interpreted the nondiscrimination policy set forth in the special education legislation to mean that tests must be presented in the primary language or mode of communication of the child, and no one test or procedure can be used as the sole determinant of a child's education program.

The Educational Testing Service (ETS) recognized the need to fully consider the unique characteristics of special populations at every stage of an assessment program: design and development, administration, interpretation, and reporting results (Mounty & Anderson, 1993). ETS established a Special Population Group to ensure that issues of access, equity, opportunity, and/or outcomes/consequences are addressed. They are studying equal opportunity for female, minority, and disabled students to have access to information, resources, state-of-the-art curricula, and educational technology pertinent to successful performance on standardized tests and large-scale assessment. All types of validity are enhanced by studying differential performance, fairness in testing practices for improved equity, the equalization of access to educational opportunities for successful outcomes, and the use of assessment information.

How can the researcher determine the validity of proposed measurement procedures? We discuss four specific approaches to establishing validity (content, concurrent, predictive, and construct validity).

Content Validity. If the purpose of the test is to measure the effect of a specific teaching strategy or curricula, then the researcher can establish content validity by determining if the knowledge, skill, or attitude measured by the test matches the information included in the lessons actually taught. A specifications matrix, which crosses the items of the measurement device and the objectives of the lesson or curriculum, can be helpful in establishing content validity. The higher the degree of overlap, the more the measure can be said to have content validity.

Use of minimum competency tests with students with disabilities provides one example of problems with content validity in special education. Minimum competency tests are used to measure attainment of mastery of skills and competencies, usually for the purpose of determining promotion to the next grade or awarding a high school diploma. In a case heard before the Federal District Court in the state of Georgia, it was found that children with mental retardation were not instructed on the skills tested on a diploma sanction test (*Anderson v. Banks*, 1981, cited in Thurlow et al., 1993). Thus, the test did not have content validity for these students. Some students can succeed with the same content, but need modifications in the testing process. Others may have different instructional goals, often focusing on lower levels of skill development. The content validity of the tests should be checked against the student's instructional goals on the IEP. An alternative to minimum competency testing is to examine accomplishment of goals as specified on the IEP (Thurlow et al., 1993). This results in data that is quite complex and variable, and thus interpretation would be difficult across subjects or groups.

Concurrent Validity. Tests are sometimes used in place of ratings of demonstrations of skills or knowledge in an educational or work environment. A test is said to have concurrent validity if it yields results similar to those obtained from assessment of the actual performance of the skill or task. Certification and licensure tests are used to determine whether individuals have the needed skills and knowledge to assume a professional role. Thurlow et al. (1993) summarized the modifications that ETS has made in the National Teachers' Exam to accommodate persons with disabilities.

Predictive Validity. Often the researcher wants to use the information derived from the administration of an instrument to predict a subject's performance at some future point in time. For example, the research project might be designed to develop an instrument to predict the level of success students with disabilities will have in postsecondary training experiences. Although time-consuming, the typical approach to establishing the predictive validity of a measurement technique is to administer the test, wait until the predicted behavior occurs, and correlate measures of this behavior with the student's performance on the original test.

A study by the American College Testing (ACT) Program (Laing & Farmer, 1984) compared the predictive validity of the ACT for five groups of examinees: students with and without disabilities who took the exam in a standard administration, and students with visual impairments, hearing impairments, or motor disabilities (defined as physical and learning disabilities) who took a nonstandard administration. The ability of the exam to predict first-year college grades (the criterion measure) was about the same for examinees with and without disabilities when both groups took the exam under standard testing conditions. Similar results were also reported by ETS on the Scholastic Aptitude Test and the Graduate Record Exam (Willingham, Ragosta, Bennett, Braun, Rock, & Powers, 1988). However, test scores substantially underpredicted college grades for students with hearing impairments who enrolled in colleges that provided them with special services.

Construct Validity. Finally, the researcher who wants to measure some attribute, such as intelligence or anxiety, must establish construct validity, that is, provide evidence that the test actually measures the intended construct and not some other characteristic, such as lack of access to information because of bias based on gender, ethnicity, class, or disability.

Language from Section 504 of the Vocational Rehabilitation Act (1973) reflects the concern for construct validity in Section 84.42 (b)(3), which states:

> . . . admissions tests are selected and administered so as best to ensure that, when a test is administered to an applicant who has a handicap that impairs sensory, manual, or speaking skills, the test results accurately reflect the applicant's aptitude or achievement level or whatever other factor the test purports to measure, rather than reflecting the applicant's impaired sensory, manual, or speaking skills (except where those skills are the factors that the test purports to measure).

In other words, the test must be validated to reflect the applicant's aptitude and achievement, rather than any disability extraneous to what is being measured.

Objectivity

In some research situations, the measurement instrument is a person who serves as an interviewer, observer, or reviewer of documents. When the instrument is a human, users of the research findings are likely to challenge the results by asking: Are these data independent of the person doing the observations? Would another person come to the same conclusions? Would the observer have seen things the same way at a later date? All these concerns relate to fluctuations in the measurement resulting from the subjectivity of the task of observation.

In response to these concerns, the researcher must first establish that the tasks the observer is required to do are valid for the purposes of the research. For example, if the research was intended to describe the social skills of students with learning disabilities, then the researcher would have to present evidence that the observer was looking for essential indicators of social skills. Next, the researcher would gather evidence that the observation task was objective, that more than one observer could look at the same behaviors and reach the same interpretation. The researcher might train two or more observers on the observation scheme and compare their observations. This is usually referred to as *interrater reliability,* because the purpose is to check the consistency of ratings across observers. Correlations of ratings or percent of agreement are two methods for establishing interrater reliability.

Finally, the researcher should check for fluctuations in rating across time, because raters may change as they become more involved with the rating task. They may get better, or they may get tired or bored. Regardless of the reason, their ratings change and result in different interpretations of the same data. In this case it is important to conduct *intrarater reliability* studies. Again, percent of agreement within individual rater, and correlations of observations across time, are two methods for determining intrarater reliability. McIntosh, Vaughn, Hager, and Okhee (1993) trained observers to study the integration of students with learning disabilities in general education classrooms. They used random checks of observers throughout the data collection to insure inter- and intrarater reliability.

Test Modifications and Technical Adequacy

When tests or testing procedures are modified, questions are raised about the technical adequacy (reliability/validity) of the modified tests

(Thurlow et al., 1993). Tests and other evaluation materials are only valid and reliable when used with the same population on which they were developed, for the specific purpose for which they were developed, and when following the same procedures used in development.

The American Psychological Association's *Standards for Educational and Psychological Testing* (1985) succinctly identified problems concerning the impact of modification of tests on their technical adequacy. Standard 6.2 states:

> When a test user makes a substantial change in test format, mode of administration, instruction, language or content, the user should revalidate the use of the test for the changed conditions or have a rationale supporting the claims that additional validation is not necessary or possible. (p. 41)

SELECTING AND USING A MEASUREMENT DEVICE

The researcher has two choices with regard to the measurement procedures: (1) Measures may be selected from those that are currently available commercially or those that have been developed by other researchers. (2) If the appropriate measure cannot be found, then the researcher must adapt an existing instrument or build a new one to meet the needs of the proposed research. Development of measurement tools is beyond the scope of this text; the interested reader is referred to such sources as the American Psychological Association's *Standards for Educational and Psychology Tests* (1985), Borg and Gall (1989), and Morris, Fitz-Gibbon, and Lindheim (1987).

The researcher must remember that regardless of the direction of the decision to select, modify, or develop a measurement procedure, the quality of information generated by the use of the device is essential. According to Bennett (1983), there are three basic requirements to consider: (1) special qualifications for the persons administering the instrument; (2) the technical adequacy of the instrument for assessing the desired attributes; and (3) the extent to which the measurement is free from bias based on gender, ethnicity, class, or disability. These features of the measure have been discussed elsewhere. They are presented here as broad guidelines for the researcher who is searching for the appropriate tools. Deficiencies in any of the three areas will affect the quality of information available to answer the research questions.

Unfortunately, as Bennett noted, information about these features is not likely to be readily available, particularly for assessments used with persons with disabilities.

The first step in identifying a measurement device for your research is to obtain an information base of all possible existing measures that might be appropriate for your study. There are numerous resources to support this search. As noted in Chapter 2, the current literature is a good starting place. The researcher can locate and review similar research to gain an understanding of which measurement procedures worked well in other related research. In addition to reviewing specific research, the search can be extended to test bibliographic resources such as the *Mental Measurements Yearbooks*, Volumes 1-10 (e.g., Conoley & Kramer, 1989) or *Test Critiques*, Volumes 1-8 (e.g., Keyser & Sweetland, 1991). Thousands of tests are reviewed in these bibliographies. Reviews include not only general test information, but also critiques of the measurement device by experts in the field. Reliability and validity studies also are likely to be cited. Most university libraries contain numerous test bibliographies.

Selecting an instrument is guided by one broad criterion: *relevance*. The relevance question has two parts. First, to what extent is the test under consideration appropriate for the information needs of the proposed research? Of course this is a validity question, and the answer will be found in validity studies for the test being considered. The essential concern for the researcher is the degree of match between the information that will be provided through the administration and the research question being addressed in the research.

The second aspect of the relevance question focuses on the subjects of the intended research. Earlier, we noted that researchers who are reviewing potential standardized tests must be careful to note whether the test was standardized on a norm group that included persons with disabilities like those targeted in the proposed research. If not, then the norms for the test should not be used. Of greater importance, though, is the appropriateness of the tasks or items in the measurement device for the subjects in the proposed study.

We also indicated previously that a critical concern of measurement is acquiring an accurate representation of the attribute being measured. When information is collected from persons with disabilities, we must be certain that the person's disability does not mask the individual's actual level or amount of the attribute. For example, if we were attempting to measure the aptitude of persons with visual impairments, then we would need to use tasks or items that did not depend on vision. Not doing so would yield an inaccurate measure of aptitude. What we would get is a measure of visual skill as well as aptitude. The importance of taking the characteristics of the administration and content of the measurement device is discussed again in the section of this chapter centering on the use of measurement procedures in research.

Other selection criteria that should be considered include the test format and time for administration. To what extent do these features of the intended test promote or restrict accuracy of assessment of the subjects in the proposed research? Researchers who use modifications in tests or testing processes should ask themselves these questions (based on Thurlow et al., 1993):

- How should eligibility for accommodation be determined?
- What modifications should be allowed?
- Do scores achieved under nonstandard conditions have the same meaning?
- If there is a difference in performance levels between standard and non-standard administrations, are these due to actual differences in the construct being measured, or are they artifacts of modifications of the testing process?

If modifications are made, they should be assessed from the standpoint of the degree to which they violate previous assumptions about the measurement. Field tests of the instrument provide an opportunity to make such judgments. The researcher should then identify the ways in which previous assumptions about the procedures were affected.

When selecting a measurement device for your research, then, the relevance of the instrument for your intended information needs, as well as the subjects in the study, must be determined. We recommend constructing a specifications matrix which lists all the relevant criteria (both informational and subject-oriented) in the right-hand column, and then the potential instruments across the top. At the intersect of each test and criterion, the test is rated for its appropriateness. For most commercially available tests, the researcher can obtain a specimen set, which will contain copies of the test and a test manual that describes administration and scoring procedures. Often the manual will contain discussions of validity and reliability as well as considerations for using the instrument for diverse groups, including persons with disabilities. Useful procedures for selecting a measurement device appropriate to the needs of the researcher are presented in Morris et al. (1987).

Tests do not work the same for all populations and in all test circumstances. Therefore, we recommend that at a minimum, researchers gather reliability information for the specific persons studied in the research. Further, to increase the validity of the information, we recommend that multiple measures be used. Thus, if achievement is the focus of the research, the investigator might collect not only paper-and-pencil test data but also work samples, as well as performance in other settings. If researchers are attempting to determine social skill development in students with learning disabilities, they could use direct observation; personal interviews with the subject, peers, and significant others; as well as reviews of performance reports. Using more than one measurement procedure for gathering evidence in a study increases the dependability of the findings, conclusions, and recommendations.

QUESTIONS FOR CRITICALLY ANALYZING INFORMATION COLLECTION STRATEGIES AND INSTRUMENTS

1. What reliability, validity, and, if appropriate, objectivity indices are available to support the use of the proposed measurement process?
2. Are the procedures used by test developers to establish reliability, validity, and objectivity appropriate for the intended use of the proposed measurement technique? Was the research instrument developed and validated with representatives of both sexes, and diverse ethnic and disability groups?
3. Is the proposed measurement tool appropriate for the subjects and conditions of the proposed research?
4. What measurements are required to collect information on the research process?
5. When and from whom is it best to collect information, given the research questions of the proposed research?
6. Does the instrument contain language that is biased, based on gender, ethnicity, class, or disability?

QUESTIONS AND ACTIVITIES FOR DISCUSSION AND APPLICATION

1. Discuss the purpose of information collection in research settings.
2. Locate a commercially developed measure and review the manual to determine how the developers have treated the concepts of reliability,

validity, objectivity, and bias based on gender, ethnicity, class, and disability.

3. Review the same test to determine the extent to which it is relevant for specific populations of persons with disabilities (e.g., different types of disabilities, males and females, diverse ethnic groups).

4. Identify and review several journals in which research on persons with disabilities is reported. Read the instructions to potential authors to see what the journal editors require in the way of evidence of measurement reliability, validity, objectivity, and lack of bias based on gender, ethnicity, and disability.

5. In the same journals, review several articles to determine the ways in which the authors provide evidence of the reliability, validity, objectivity, and lack of bias for their measures. Identify the methods the authors used to ensure that their measures were not biased in that the person's disability could mask true measurement of the intended attributes.

6. Discuss the relative merits of using commercially developed measures and those developed specifically for the purposes of the proposed research.

7. Identify attributes of persons with disabilities that might be the focus of research and determine several different ways in which each attribute might be measured.

8. Identify the alternative sources from which existing information could be collected about students with disabilities that could have a bearing on a particular research initiative.

9. Identify an attribute that might be measured in a research setting. Develop a draft measurement procedure, using the steps outlined in this chapter.

10. Select a commercial instrument or one developed by another researcher and discuss modifications that may be needed for students with disabilities. Which would invalidate the technical adequacy of the test and which would not?

7

Data Analysis, Interpretation, and Reporting

Data analysis procedures are tools we use to interpret the data collected as part of the research process. Statistics are tools for information reduction that summarize characteristics or performance data in a quantitative way to ease interpretation of the results. Codes, categories, and theoretical models are ways of summarizing and interpreting qualitative data. We now look at data analysis, interpretation, and reporting in the special education context.

In This Chapter

- Challenges in data analysis and interpretation for quantitative research studies are described.
- Analysis and interpretation issues for qualitative research studies are discussed.
- Issues related to reporting results are also included.
- Questions for critically analyzing data analysis and interpretation in research studies are provided.

QUANTITATIVE DATA ANALYSIS

It is not possible to either define all the statistical terms or explain all the complexity of formula derivation and use of statistics in such a chapter as this. It is not even possible to introduce all the different kinds of statistics, or to make it clear when it is appropriate to use which one. The reader is referred to general statistics books for more specific information on this topic (see Hays, 1988; Heiman, 1992; Popham & Sirotnik, 1992).

This chapter focuses on the challenges special educators face in data analysis and interpretation. A study of integrating students with disabilities into mainstream classrooms is used to illustrate these challenges (and ways to meet those challenges) for the interpretation of quantitative data (see Table 7.1).

Table 7.1

Sample Research Study for Statistical Analysis Applications

Fuchs, Fuchs, and Fernstrom (1992) addressed the problem of reintegrating special education students into mainstream classrooms. Their purpose was to implement and validate a process by which pupils with mild and moderate disabilities (learning disabilities, behavior disorders, and language impairments) could be transitioned into regular math education classes. Their *experimental treatment* was a process for readying students to transition, using a curriculum-based measurement system that included goal setting, repeated measurement on goal material, feedback to the teachers to adjust their instructional programs, and transenvironmental programming that included skill training for the transitioning student. Their dependent variables included math achievement scores, time spent in special education math, and teachers' ratings of the students and the program. They had three groups of students: students in special education math classes who received the *experimental treatment* and were transitioned into regular math classes; *control students* in special education math classes who did not receive the treatment and followed the school's typical process for reintegration; and *Low Achieving Peers (LAPs)* who were identified by their teachers as representing their lowest acceptable math group in the regular math classroom.

Based on statistical analysis, the authors concluded that the experimental students' pre- to posttreatment performance improved significantly as compared to the control group. Further analysis indicated that the experimental group's improvement occurred while the students were in the experimental treatment condition (i.e., preparing for transition), and that their progress ceased after they entered the regular education classes.

CHALLENGES IN ANALYSIS AND INTERPRETATION

Randomization and sample size are two factors that present challenges to special education researchers who plan to use statistical procedures for data analysis. Following a discussion of these two factors, we present options for researchers to deal with these challenges.

Randomization

Randomization is a necessary condition for the use of typical tests of parametric statistics, for example, *t*-test, ANOVA (Shaver, 1992). Randomness can be achieved by either random sampling (Chapter 5) or random assignment to conditions (Chapter 3). Random sampling is a very difficult condition to meet in most education research (it was not achieved in the Fuchs, Fuchs, & Fernstrom, 1992, study), and random assignment is not always possible or legal. For example, Fuchs et al. were able to randomly assign 13 subjects to their experimental group and 13 to their control group (26 out of a pool of 42). They obviously could not assign LAP students, because that was an extant condition. The research team reported results separately for the randomly assigned subset and for the total sample. Fortunately for them, the results were the same for both analyses.

Sample Size

Sample size is a basic influence on statistical significance (Thompson, 1992). Virtually any study can have statistically significant results if a large enough sample size is used. For example, with a standard deviation of 10 and a sample size of 20, a difference of 9.4 between two independent means is necessary for statistical significance at the .05 level in a nondirectional test; with a sample size of 100, a difference of only 4.0 is required, and with a sample size of 1000, a difference of only 1.2 is required (Shaver, 1992). An overly large sample size was not a problem in the Fuchs et al. (1992) study; however, it could be a problem in special education research (see Allen, 1992). More commonly, a very small sample size might prevent the researcher from obtaining statistically significant results.

As was mentioned in Chapter 5, it is often appropriate to report results in a disaggregated mode, for example, to report results by gender, ethnicity, or type of disability. In such cases, the researcher must have selected a large enough sample to make the disaggregation meaningful.

RESPONSES TO ANALYSIS AND INTERPRETATION CHALLENGES

Suggestions for dealing with these challenges include: (1) choose a different statistic (e.g., effect size or nonparametric statistics), (2) change the design to include plans for replication, and (3) discuss competing explanations and limitations of the study in the report.

Choice of a Statistic

Effect Size. Shaver (1992) and Carver (1992) recommend that researchers report their effect sizes rather than statistical significance when that is inappropriate. For studies that use means to compare an experimental and control group, the effect size is defined as the distance between the two group means in terms of their common standard deviation (Cooper, 1989). Thus, an effect size of .5 means that the two means are separated by one half a standard deviation. This is a way of describing how well the average student who received the treatment performed, relative to the average student who did not receive the treatment. For example, if an experimental group of students with behavioral problems received a drug treatment and the control group received a placebo, an effect size of .8 would indicate that the experimental group's mean was .8 standard deviation above the control group.

Snyder and Lawson (1992) warn against a blind interpretation of effect size based on magnitude, and suggest that the judgment of significance rests with the researcher's, user's, and reviewer's personal value systems; the research questions posed; societal concerns; and the design of a particular study. For more detailed information on effect size, the reader is referred to Lipsey (1990).

Nonparametric Statistics. Nonparametric statistics provide an alternative for researchers when their data do not meet the basic assumption of normality, or they have small samples, or they use data of an ordinal or nominal nature.

Design Considerations: Replication

Carver (1992) recommends the replication of studies' results as the best replacement for statistical significance. Building replication into research helps eliminate chance or sampling error as a threat to the internal validity of the results. This also emphasizes the importance of the literature review, as was discussed in Chapter 2. Because the Fuchs et al. results were based on 13 students who were reintegrated into mainstream classes, it would strengthen their claims to see the study replicated.

Competing Explanations

As was discussed in the chapter on quantitative research methods, the researcher needs to consider competing explanations (threats to internal and external validity). Such competing explanations become critical when it is time to interpret the results. For example, Fuchs et al. described efforts they made to determine whether initial differences existed between the groups. They administered Stanford Achievement Test Applications and Computation subtests to the three groups and, using ANOVA, concluded that the groups did not differ initially. They also disaggregated the three groups, with respect to race, grade level, and gender, and found them to be similar. They did not address the difference in disabilities in terms of the groups.

Recognizing Limitations

As should be clear by now, it is not possible to design and conduct the "perfect" research study in special education. Therefore, it is incumbent upon the researcher to recognize and discuss the limitations of the study. For example, Fuchs et al. recognized that educators in their study were volunteers, and therefore represented a self-selected group. The choice of students for reintegration candidates was based on the personal judgment of the special educators, and therefore might be difficult to replicate in another setting. Finally, the lack of progress of the reintegrated students must be looked at seriously. Is it progress to move students into a mainstream classroom if their academic progress stops? What happened in the mainstream classroom that led to this condition? The Fuchs et al. study was not designed to answer such questions, but a qualitative research study could be designed to that purpose.

QUALITATIVE DATA ANALYSIS
AND INTERPRETATION

Data analysis in qualitative studies designed within the ethnographic or phenomenological traditions occurs throughout the study. Analysis is recursive; findings are generated and systematically built as successive pieces of data are gathered (Stainback & Stainback, 1988).

The actual mechanics of qualitative data analysis are beyond the scope of this text. The reader is referred to Miles and Huberman (1984) for a logical positivist approach to qualitative data analysis that results in data displays such as graphs, charts, matrices, and networks. Many texts are available that describe the ethnographic/phenomenological approach to data analysis (Bogdan & Biklen, 1992; Fetterman, 1989; Guba & Lincoln, 1989; Patton, 1990; Tesch, 1990). Tesch (1989, 1990) provides a description of computerized analysis of qualitative data.

Based on a qualitative analysis of texts that describe qualitative principles and procedures, Tesch (1990) identified principles and practices that hold true for most types of qualitative research analysis and interpretation. The special education researcher should be aware of the following principles and practices in qualitative data analysis:

One: Analysis occurs throughout the data collection process. Stainback and Stainback (1988) identified different levels of data analysis that occur during the course of a study. Initially, while the researcher is in the field, he or she reflects on impressions, relationships, patterns, commonalities, and the like. For example, during a study of special education training in Egypt, Mertens (1993a) shared the results of her initial impressions with participants who were deaf, blind, or nondisabled on a daily basis. This allowed the participants to be informed of any hypotheses that the researcher was formulating, and to add their own interpretations to the data. The second level of analysis occurs when the researcher sits down to organize and develop the variety of data collected in the field to develop detailed notes. The researcher analyzes the logic and the correspondence of data to initial impressions in the field. Periodically throughout the study, the researcher carefully and thoroughly studies all the data, seeking similarities, differences, correspondence, categories, themes, concepts and ideas, and analyzes the logic of previous analytic outcomes, categories, and weaknesses or gaps in the data. Some methodologists recommend that the researcher wait for up to one month before conducting the final analysis of the data in order to gain a fresh perspective on the nature of the data and the problems (Bogdan & Biklen, 1992; Stainback & Stainback, 1988).

Two: "The analysis process is systematic and comprehensive, but not rigid" (Tesch, 1990, p. 95). Unlike quantitative statistical analysis, there is no test of statistical significance to tell the researcher that the data analysis is at an end. Lincoln and Guba (1985) recommend that the data analysis be stopped with the emergence of regularities, that is, no new information is emerging with additional data analysis.

Three: Data analysis includes reflective activities that result in a set of notes that record the analytic process, thus providing accountability. Procedures (also discussed in Chapter 4) include the inquiry audit in which an "auditor" examines the fairness of the research process and the accuracy of the product in terms of internal coherence and support by data (Lincoln & Guba, 1985). Keller (1993) used peer debriefing in his case study of a girl with Down syndrome, by exposing his research findings to an uninvolved peer. Outside referees can be asked to review the data analysis procedures and results.

Four: The analysis process begins with reading all the data at once and then dividing the data into smaller, more meaningful units. For example, in Mertens's (1992) study of contextual factors that influence the success of total inclusion program planning, she identified such categories as the state's Least Restrictive Environment policy, the quality of existing services, the strength of advocacy groups, the process of communicating information to parents and staff, and the number and characteristics of the students involved.

Five: The data segments are organized into a system that is predominantly derived from the data; that is, the data analysis process is inductive. Some guiding research questions can be formulated at the beginning of the process; however, additional categories or themes are allowed to emerge from the data. In the total inclusion study, Mertens (1992) used a semistructured interview guide, based on previous research on factors that influence the success of total inclusion programs. However, the participants were first asked an open-ended question about advice they would give to others who might want to implement a total inclusion program.

Six: The main analytic process is comparison, that is, the researcher uses comparison to build and refine categories, define conceptual similarities, find negative evidence, and discover patterns. Mertens (1992) discovered that a top-down approach to implementing a total inclusion program created more negative feelings than a shared governance approach. Other problems were common to all the schools studied, such as the need for additional training and support staff; however, the feelings expressed by students, parents, and staff were more negative in the top-down schools.

Seven: The categories are flexible and are modified as further data analysis occurs. For example, a researcher might start with a category called "finances," and find later that it is more functional to divide that category into "current finances" and "future financial needs."

Eight: Qualitative data analysis is neither scientific nor mechanistic. The basis for judging the quality of analysis in a qualitative study rests on corroboration, to be sure that the research findings reflect people's perceptions (Stainback and Stainback, 1988). Several of the criteria for judging the quality of qualitative studies in general, which were presented in Chapter 4, have relevance for the quality of the data analysis in particular. Specifically, triangulation requires the convergence of multiple data sources from a variety of participants under a variety of conditions. It should be noted that all people and sources may not agree, and this difference in opinion should be made explicit in the report.

Nine: The result of an analysis is some type of higher-order synthesis in the form of a descriptive picture, patterns, or themes, or emerging or substantive theory. The results of the study of total inclusion planning processes consisted of a framework for decisions related to implementing a program to bring students with disabilities into their neighborhood schools (Mertens, 1992). Factors that were identified fit in the following broad categories: planning and contextual factors, parental involvement, training, logistics, curriculum issues, and spill-over effects.

REPORTING RESEARCH

Researchers have a wide range of options available to them for reporting their research, such as memos, presentations at professional meetings, journal articles, and technical reports. Typically, a research report includes an introduction (with a literature review), method, results, and discussion. The exact structure differs, depending on the type of research (quantitative/qualitative), the audience, and the purpose of the report. Research reports can have multiple uses for different audiences; thus, alternative reporting formats should be considered for dissemination.

In both quantitative and qualitative studies, the researcher should tie the results back to the purpose for the study, and to the literature in the discussion section of the report. Further, findings should be based on data, and caution should be exercised in recommendations for practice.

Quantitative reports typically report results using tables and graphs. They also tend to use a detached style, avoiding the use of the first person and employing the passive voice. While qualitative reports can use tables and graphs (Miles & Huberman, 1984), they typically present results in a more narrative style, and include more personal revelations about the author (Van Maanen, 1988).

In qualitative reports, Stainback and Stainback (1988) recommend that the reader look for a deep and valid description, and well-grounded hypotheses and theories that emerge from a wide variety of data gathered over an extended period of time. The researcher should also seek contextual meaning, that is, attempt to understand the social and cultural context of the situation in which the statements are made and the behaviors exhibited. This includes a description of relevant contextual variables such as home, community, history, educational background, physical arrangements, emotional climate, and rules.

QUESTIONS FOR CRITICALLY ANALYZING DATA ANALYSIS AND INTERPRETATION

Quantitative Research

(Note: The reader is referred to the general statistical texts referenced at the beginning of this chapter for an explanation of the statistical terms and concepts used in these questions.)

1. What types of statistical analysis were used? Were they appropriate to the level of measurement, hypotheses, and the design of the study? What alpha level was used to determine statistical significance?
2. Is there statistical significance? What was the effect size?
3. Does the researcher interpret significance tests correctly (i.e., avoid saying the results were highly significant or approached significance)?
4. When the sample size is small and the effect size large, are the results underinterpreted? Or, if the sample size is large and effect sizes modest, are the results overinterpreted?
5. Are many univariate tests of significance used when a multivariate test would be more appropriate?
6. Are basic assumptions for parametric, inferential statistics met (i.e., normal distribution, level of measurement and randomization)?

(Note: Criteria 3 through 6 were adapted from Thompson, 1988.)

Qualitative Research

1. Did regularities emerge from the data such that addition of new information would not change the results?
2. Was there corroboration between the reported results and people's perceptions? Was triangulation used? Were differences of opinions made explicit?

3. Was an audit used to determine the fairness of the research process and the accuracy of the product in terms of internal coherence and support by data?
4. Was peer debriefing used? Outside referees? Negative case analysis? Member checks?
5. Is the report long and rambling, thus making the findings unclear to the reader?
6. Was the correct conclusion missed by premature closure, resulting in superficial or wrong interpretations?
7. Did the researcher provide sufficient description?

Interpretation Issues

1. How do you account for the results? What are the competing explanations; how did the authors deal with them? What competing explanations can you think of, other than those the author discussed?
2. How would the results be influenced if applied to different subjects (e.g., rural or urban)?
3. What were the processes that caused the outcomes?
4. What conclusions and/or interpretations are made? Are they appropriate to the sample, type of study, duration of the study, and findings? Does the author over/undergeneralize the results?
5. Is enough information given so that an independent researcher could replicate the study?
6. Does the researcher relate the results to the hypotheses, objectives, and other literature?
7. Does the researcher overconclude? Are the conclusions supported by the results?
8. What extraneous variables might have affected the outcomes of this study? Does the author mention them? What were the controls? Were they sufficient?
9. Did the author acknowledge the limitations of the study?

QUESTIONS AND ACTIVITIES FOR DISCUSSION AND APPLICATION

1. How can sample size influence statistical significance? Why is this particularly important in special education research?
2. Why is randomization important in choice of statistical test? Why is this particularly important for special education research?

3. What can a researcher do when the basic assumptions for parametric inferential statistics are not met?

4. Answer the questions for critical analysis of data analysis and interpretation in quantitative research and for interpretation issues for the following study:

Example: The National Longitudinal Transition Study (NLTS) of Special Education Students findings demonstrated that young women with disabilities had a pattern of experience in early years after secondary school that differed significantly from that of men (Wagner, 1992). Females were significantly less involved in employment and other productive activities outside the home and also had less social involvement. The data indicate that females in secondary special education were more seriously impaired than their male peers. The authors explored a number of competing explanations. For example, do disabilities occur more frequently among males? Or, are learning disabilities more frequently ignored in females? Also, females were significantly less likely to have taken occupationally specific vocational training. Finally, females with disabilities were more likely to become mothers (and particularly single mothers) in the early years after leaving school.

5. What is the basis for judging the quality of data analysis and interpretation in qualitative research?

6. Answer the questions for critically analyzing data analysis and interpretation in qualitative research and interpretation issues for the following study:

Example: This case study examined the integration of autistic students in a high school setting (Ferguson, 1992). The researcher gathered data over a 4-month period. Initially, the observations lasted between 1 and 2 hours and occurred once or twice a week across a variety of settings and time. Gradually, the visits became less frequent and were interspersed with interviews of teachers, administrators, support staff, and students. The autistic students spend most of their time apart from typical students, in a self-contained classroom. Only two of the students go out for any classes. Integration in the shop class and home economics class works because the special education teacher accompanies the students and adapts the materials for them. The students are nonverbal and thus are not actively disruptive.

8

Future Directions for Special Education Research

In This Chapter

- Substantive and methodological issues for the future of special education research are discussed.

Emerging trends in special education create a need for an increased knowledge base. While future directions for special education research are divided into substantive and methodological issues, in some sense this is an artificial distinction, because the substantive issue in part determines the appropriate methodological approach. Nevertheless, this approach allows a distinction between issues for which more research is needed, and emerging approaches that can be used to address those issues.

SUBSTANTIVE ISSUES

The underlying issue in special education is how to bring about real change in the delivery of special education and related services to persons with special needs. Ysseldyke, Algozzine, and Thurlow (1992) suggest that real change will not occur unless power relationships in the classrooms and schools are modified, allowing for meaningful participation on the part of workers in decisions about the quality of their work and the time needed to complete it. We discuss a number of emerging trends in special education that need additional research, but the reader is cautioned to realize that change in these areas is not an isolated affair. Without structural changes in power relationships, action on the other issues will be but a Band-Aid on a festering sore.

Many substantive issues for the future of special education were identified by a survey conducted, by the Federal Resource Center for Special Education, of knowledgeable representatives of the field (e.g., government administrators, school personnel, and private practitioners such as advocates) (Hales & Carlson, 1992). Respondents were asked to rate almost 200 statements as to their likelihood and desirability of occurrence for special education in the future. Results of this survey are integrated into this section on substantive issues.

Early Intervention

The legislative changes in special education for infants and children (ages birth to 5 years) create a need for additional research in the areas of identification, referral, and service delivery with this population (Hart, 1990; U.S. Department of Education, 1991). Research is needed regarding the efficacy of early interventions, ways to work with parents and families, and personnel preparation. The respondents in the Federal Resource Center survey indicated an increasing likelihood that research will focus on early identification and diagnosis of emotional problems of infants and toddlers as a preventative intervention (Hales & Carlson, 1992).

Educational Processes and Options

A myriad of educational issues emerge from trends in special education, including the efficacy of alternative school placements, vocational training, community-based training, independent living skills, preparation for life, functional skill training, adjustment to adult life, privatization and choice, provision of service models (such as consultation, interagency cooperation, collaboration between general and special educators), use of technology, working with families, referral policies and practices, prereferral strategies, teaching social skills, and subject specific areas such as literacy, English language development, and science.

In the Federal Resource Center study (Hales & Carlson, 1992), the following substantive areas related to curriculum and instruction were identified:

1. Instruction will occur increasingly in natural environments, with a focus on individualized instructional objectives rather than the student's particular diagnosed disability.
2. Cooperative learning approaches will be used to a greater extent with students both with and without disabilities.
3. Students with disabilities and their families will play a more significant role in decision making about special education programs.

Inclusion

As a press for total inclusion is felt, the question that arises is: What really happens to children with special learning needs in the regular classroom? (See, e.g., Fuchs, Fuchs, & Fernstrom, 1992.) Gallagher (1990) raised other questions, including:

1. How do you address the attitudinal factor as it plays in the resistance to integration?
2. How do you account for the tremendous range of individual differences at any one age level? ("How can a single teacher, even with help, take care of children with this range of performance and ability?") (p. 49).
3. What are the structural properties of an integrated educational system?
4. What evidence is there that the life of the child is improved by integration?

Gallagher noted that education is not designed to prepare everyone to do the same thing in the future. He asked at what point in the educational stream there should be differential channels. He described the dilemma as one of how to integrate and diversify. He stated, "We should now be entering an era where objective data takes the place of rhetoric. . . . It is not enough to point to the shortcomings of the existing system . . . we need more evidence of the virtues of the 'new movement' " (p. 36).

Specific Disabling Conditions

The emergence of new classifications for disabling conditions, such as crack babies, ADD, ADHA, and traumatic brain injuries, creates a need for additional research on these populations. Other populations in need of special services may be expected to emerge as medical advances result in saving the lives of children who have severe medical problems. Many of the issues that have been discussed cut across disabling conditions; however, research needs have been identified for specific disability areas, and the reader is referred to Scholl (1990) for information on blindness, Hart (1990) on infants with disabilities, Fischgrund (1990) on deafness, Keough (1990) on learning disabilities, Wood (1990) on serious emotional disturbance, Reschly (1990) on mental retardation, Haring and Laitinen (1992) on severe disabilities, Koppenhaver and Yoder (1992) on severe speech and physical impairments, and Aarons and Gittens (1992) on autism. In a survey of special education divisions in state departments of education, the disabling conditions that were mentioned as being most in need of additional attention included serious emotional disturbance, severe mental retardation, and deaf-blindness (U.S. Department of Education, 1991). In addition, those surveyed cited a need for additional information on how best to serve minority and bilingual populations with disabilities. Within specific disabling conditions, additional information is needed concerning their characteristics and developmental trends.

Training

With the emergence of early intervention and other new classifications, modification in training of professional personnel is needed. One of the strongest predictions resulting from the Federal Resource Center survey identified a critical shortage of special education personnel at all levels (Hales & Carlson, 1992). Researchers can contribute to the identification of new and more effective recruitment strategies, including recruitment of individuals from culturally, racially, ethnically, and linguistically diverse backgrounds. This predicted shortage of personnel could result in an increasing role for paraprofessionals.

Other training implications include preparation of general education teachers to serve students with mild disabilities, thus blurring the line between special and general education. This would require investigation of collaborative or team teaching configurations. A final implication related to the personnel shortage is investigation of alternative routes for certification of professionals. Therefore, research concerning the needed skills, and appropriateness and effectiveness of training, is needed.

School-Linked Services

The Federal Resource Center respondents predicted that related services could continue to expand in type, quality, and variety (Hales & Carlson, 1992). The increased linkages with schools and services tied to health, day care, and mental health services need to be studied in terms of their impact on resources and on students with disabilities and their families.

Women and Minorities With Disabilities

As was mentioned in Chapter 1, researchers in special education have traditionally ignored differences by gender, race, ethnicity, and social class. Asch and Fine (1992) recommended investigation of such issues as the effects of race, class, and gender on school experiences of persons with disabilities. For example, what does it mean for a mother or father, rich or poor, to have a son or daughter with a disability? When parents and teachers create individual education plans, are girls and boys with comparable impairments equally likely to be given the optimal supplemental services or the greatest opportunity for integrated classrooms and social activity? What accounts for the more negative self-perception of girls and women with disabilities, as compared to their male peers? How do some women and minorities with disabilities flourish despite pressures of family and discrimination meted out by society?

METHODOLOGICAL ISSUES

In some ways, the methodological challenges in special education are the same as those in any social science research. Switzky and Heal (1990) note the need for strategies to improve internal, external, and social validity, and for improved reliability and validity in measurement. However, they also caution that it is time to examine scientific research methods to determine how they can be applied to solve the complex special education problems.

Theoretical Frameworks

Several researchers have suggested that special education research can be improved by adapting theoretical frameworks that have developed in general education, such as in the areas of literacy (Koppenhaver & Yoder, 1992); cognitive learning theory (Mertens, 1991b); effective schools research (Wang, Reynolds, & Walberg, 1990); and cooperative learning (Slavin, 1987). As was noted in Chapter 2, the use of a theoretical framework can be useful in formulating research questions and in the interpretation of the results.

Emerging Models for Research

Skrtic (1991) claims that the problem with special education is not that it is atheoretical, but that it is acritical; that is, it operates with an implicit theory with unexamined assumptions. He says that special educators need to critically analyze the assumptions behind their practices, using critical pragmatism in order to reach a hermeneutical understanding.

This hermeneutical understanding reflects knowledge that results from coming to understand, to some degree, the knowledge traditions of other cultural groups, such as the persons with disabilities and their parents. The methodological implication of striving for hermeneutical understanding is that knowledge develops through dialogue, questioning, and conversation. This is an approach advocated by constructivists (Guba & Lincoln, 1989) and feminist researchers (Lather, 1992).

Hahn (1989) asserts that the conventional approach to research and practice in special education has been shaped by a "functional limitations" model, such that the researcher assumes that the principal difficulties of people with disabilities reside within these individuals, and the solutions can be found by surmounting or transcending such deficits. Therefore, the emphasis is on the development of effective instructional methods, rather than on the external nature of the problems. To be effective, researchers need to focus on ways to change the pervasive attitudes toward disabled persons, recognizing that all aspects of the environment are fundamentally molded by public policy, and public policy is a reflection of prevalent attitudes and values. And persons with disabilities need to develop a sense of personal and political identity to combat discrimination.

As was mentioned in Chapter 4, Peck and Furman (1992) extend this idea of a need to modify research approaches to recognize the political nature of the problems of people with disabilities. They contend that unless special education researchers turn away from the deficit-oriented approach, and adopt the use of qualitative methods, they will not ask some of the critical questions about why children are not succeeding in school.

More Specific Descriptions Needed

A pervasive problem in special (and general) education research is the lack of specificity in the description of the independent variables, contextual factors, and subject characteristics (Haring & Laitinen, 1992; Keough, 1990; Wang et al., 1990). Part of the problem arises because of inconsistencies in classification definitions for different disability areas (Reschly, 1990; Walker, Singer, Palfrey, Orza, Wenger, & Butler, 1988; Wood, 1990). Research is needed to determine the usefulness of changes in classification schemes (see Keough, 1990).

Qualitative researchers argue that the aggregation of individuals with a common label obscures the true nature of the individuals involved in the research. Qualitative approaches are designed to provide the richness of detail that would furnish a picture of the complexity of the program, the contextual factors, and the individuals involved.

Assessment

Additional research is needed on innovative assessment techniques, as well as on the effects of adapted or modified assessment strategies, within all disability areas. Innovative approaches are emerging, such as using computers for assessment, ecological appraisal, assessment of instructional environments, curriculum-based measurement, portfolio assessment, collaborative problem solving, performance-based assessment, and neuropsychological appraisal. Ysseldyke et al. (1992) were not optimistic that these innovative approaches to assessment would find their way into practice. They stated: " . . . assessment practices today look for the most part as they did in 1970, and there is little reason to believe they will change. Sure, the social, political, economic, and cultural happenings since 1970 have influenced assessment practices, but they have not led to fundamental change" (p. 365).

Statistical Techniques and Replication

As was noted in Chapter 7, statisticians are questioning the use of parametric statistics when their underlying assumptions are not met. In future research, we may find reports of effect sizes instead of statistical significance, more use of nonparametric statistics, and more emphasis on replication of results. Switzky and Heal (1990) recommended the use of more sophisticated statistical techniques such as path analysis to address the complex issues in special education; however, it is difficult to meet the assumptions that underlie such tests.

Relationship Between Researchers and Collaborators

If research is to have applicability, collaborative relationships between researchers, special educators, and people with disabilities and their parents must be strengthened. One model of collaborative research is described by Davis and Ferguson (1992): A university faculty member and a special education teacher shared the responsibility of exploring ways to empower learning disabled students in regular classrooms through a constructivist framework. Research is also needed on the best way to transfer research-based knowledge to classroom practice.

Shift or Balance?

While some researchers claim that a shift in paradigms is occurring and is necessary (Guba & Lincoln, 1989; Peck & Furman, 1992), others are calling for a more balanced approach in which educational issues can be addressed from both a positivist and a constructivist framework (Gaylord-Ross, 1990-1992; Levitan, 1992). Gaylord-Ross (1990-1992) wrote:

> While these research methods [experimental, positivist research] have led to advances in the field, the question still remains whether a research model endemic to special education will emerge. It may be asking too much to expect an applied field to generate a new model for research. Yet if the quality and contributions of an applied science are to increase, one might hope for a unique research methodology to emerge. (p. xiii)

Gaylord-Ross did not see the emergence of a new research methodology in the near future. He felt that researchers could benefit by new treatments of cumulative databases and the presenting of information from multiple sources (as was recommended in Chapter 5). It is the authors' hope that, by synthesizing the issues and methodological challenges that are either unique to or highly salient for special education, this volume will lead to an improvement of the quality of research and the lives of persons with disabilities.

References

AAMR. (1992). *Mental retardation: Definition, classification, and systems of support* (9th ed.). Washington, DC: The American Association on Mental Retardation.

Aarons, M., & Gittens, T. (1992). *The handbook of autism*. New York: Routledge.

Allen, T. E. (1992). Subgroup differences in educational placement for deaf and hard of hearing students in the United States, *American Annals of the Deaf, 137*(5), 381-388.

American Psychological Association. (1985). *Standards for educational and psychological testing*. Washington, DC: Author.

Andrews, J. F., & Mason, J. M. (1986). How do deaf children learn about prereading? *American Annals of the Deaf, 131*(3), 210-216.

Ary, D., Jacobs, L. C., & Razavieh, A. (1990). *Introduction to research in education*. Fort Worth, TX: Holt, Rinehart & Winston.

Asch, A., & Fine, M. (1992). Beyond pedestals: Revisiting the lives of women with disabilities. In M. Fine (Ed.), *Disruptive voices: The possibilities of feminist research* (pp. 139-172). Ann Arbor: University of Michigan Press.

Barlow, D. H., & Hersen, M. (1984). *Single-case experimental designs: Strategies for studying behavior change*. New York: Pergamon.

Bear, G. G., Clever, A., & Proctor, W. A. (1991). Self-perceptions of nonhandicapped children and children with learning disabilities in integrated classes. *The Journal of Special Education, 24*(4), 409-426.

Beirne-Smith, M. (1991). Peer tutoring in arithmetic for children with learning disabilities. *Exceptional Children, 57*(4), 330-337.

Bennett, R. E. (1983). A multi-method approach to assessment in special education. *Diagnostique, 8*, 88-97.

Bennett, R. E., & Ragosta, M. (1988). Handicapped people. In W. W. Willingham, M. Ragosta, R. E. Bennett, H. Braun, D. A. Rock, & D. A. Powers (Eds.), *Testing handicapped people* (pp. 17-36). Boston: Allyn & Bacon.

Berk, R. A. (1986). *Performance assessment: Methods and applications*. Baltimore: The Johns Hopkins University Press.

Bigge, J. L. (1988). *Curriculum-based instruction for special education students*. Mountain View, CA: Mayfield.

Biklen, D., Ferguson, D. L., & Ford, A. (Eds.). (1989). *Schooling and disabilities* (National Society for the Study of Education yearbook series, Vol. 88). Chicago: University of Chicago Press.

Bogdan, R. C., & Biklen, S. K. (1992). *Qualitative research for education* (2nd ed.). Boston: Allyn & Bacon.

Borg, W. R., & Gall, M. D. (1989). *Educational research*. White Plains, NY: Longman.

Bowe, F. G. (1991). Access to tele-communications: The views of blind and visually impaired adults. *Journal of Visual Impairment and Blindness, 85*(8), 328-331.

Bracht, G. H., & Glass, G. V. (1968). The external validity of experiments. *American Educational Research Journal, 5*(4), 437-474.

Bruininks, R. H., & Thurlow, M. L. (1988). *Evaluating post-school transition of secondary students with moderate to severe handicaps (final report)*. Minneapolis: University of Minnesota, University Affiliated Program.

Buchanan, N. K., & Feldhusen, J. F. (Eds.). (1991). *Conducting research and evaluation in gifted education*. New York: Teachers College Press.

Bullis, M., & Anderson, G. (1986). Single-subject research methodology: An underutilized tool in the field of deafness. *American Annals of the Deaf, 132*(5), 344-348.

Campbell, D. T., & Stanley, J. C. (1963). Experimental and quasi-experimental designs for research on teaching. In N. L. Gage (Ed.), *Handbook of research on teaching* (pp. 171-246). Chicago: Rand McNally.

Carver, R. P. (1992, April). *The case against statistical significance testing, revisited.* Paper presented at the annual meeting of the American Educational Research Association, San Francisco.

Cole, K. N., Mills, P. E., Dale, P. S., & Jenkins, J. R. (1991). Effects of preschool integration for children with disabilities. *Exceptional Children, 58*(1), 36-46.

Committee on Scientific and Professional Ethics and Conduct. (1981). Ethical principles of psychologists. *American Psychologist, 36*, 633-638.

Conference of Executives of American Schools for the Deaf. (1979). Suggested guidelines for research in educational programs for the deaf. *American Annals of the Deaf, 124*, 770-784.

Conoley, J. C., & Kramer, J. J. (Eds.). (1989). *Tenth mental measurements yearbook.* Lincoln: University of Nebraska-Lincoln.

Cook, J. A., & Fonow, M. M. (1990). Knowledge and women's interests: Issues of epistemology and methodology in feminist sociological research. In J. M. Nielsen (Ed.), *Feminist research methods: Exemplary readings in the social sciences* (pp. 69-93). Boulder, CO: Westview.

Cook, T. D., & Campbell, D. T. (1979). *Quasi-experimentation: Design and analysis issues for field settings*. Chicago: Rand McNally.

Cooper, H., & Hedges, L. V. (Eds.). (1994). *The handbook of research synthesis*. New York: Russell Sage.

Cooper, H. M. (1989). *Integrating research*. Newbury Park, CA: Sage.

Council for Exceptional Children. (1983). Code of ethics and standards for professional practice. *Exceptional Children, 50*, 205-209.

CRESST. (1992-1993). *The CRESST Line*. Los Angeles: UCLA.

CRESST. (1993). *Evaluation comment*. Los Angeles: UCLA.

Crowley, E. P. (1993). A qualitative analysis of mainstreamed behaviorally disordered aggressive adolescents' perceptions of helpful and unhelpful teacher attitudes and behaviors. *Exceptionality, 4*(3), 131-151.

Davila, R. R., Williams, M. L., & MacDonald, J. T. (1991, September 16). *Memo to chief state school officers*. Washington, DC: U.S. Department of Education.

Davis, C., & Ferguson, D. L. (1992). Trying something completely different: Report of a collaborative research venture. In P. M. Ferguson, D. L. Ferguson, & S. J. Taylor (Eds.), *Interpreting disability: A qualitative reader* (pp. 124-144). New York: Teachers College Press.

DeStefano, L., & Wagner, M. (1991). *Outcome assessment in special education: Lessons learned*. Menlo Park, CA: SRI International.

Ebel, R. L. (1979). *Essentials of educational measurement* (3rd ed.). Englewood Cliffs, NJ: Prentice Hall.

Edgar, E. (1988). Markers of effectiveness at the secondary level in special education. *Proceedings of the research in education of the handicapped project director's meeting.* Washington, DC: Office of Special Education Programs.

ETS. (1992). ETS conference examines the technology of computer-based testing for people with disabilities. In *ETS developments.* Princeton, NJ: Author.

FairTest. (1993). *Computerized testing: More questions than answers.* Cambridge, MA: National Center for Fair & Open Testing.

Ferguson, D. L. (1989). Severity of need and educational excellence: Public school reform and students with disabilities. In D. Biklen, D. L. Ferguson, & A. Ford (Eds.), *Schooling and disability* (National Society for the Study of Education yearbook series, Vol. 88). Chicago: University of Chicago Press.

Ferguson, P. M. (1992). The puzzle of inclusion: A case study of autistic students in the life of one high school. In P. M. Ferguson, D. L. Ferguson, & S. J. Taylor (Eds.), *Interpreting disability: A qualitative reader* (pp. 145-173). New York: Teachers College Press.

Fetterman, D. M. (1989). *Ethnography: Step by step.* Newbury Park, CA: Sage.

Finch, F. L. (Ed.). (1991). *Educational performance assessment.* Chicago: Riverside.

Fine, M., & Asch, A. (1988). Disability beyond stigma: Social interaction, discrimination, and activism. *Journal of Social Issues, 44*(1), 3-21.

Fischgrund, J. E. (1990). The education of deaf children and youth. In M. C. Wang, M. C. Reynolds, & H. J. Walberg (Eds.), *Special education: Research and practice.* Oxford, UK: Pergamon.

Fowler, F. J., Jr. (1993). *Survey research methods* (2nd ed.). Newbury Park, CA: Sage.

Fox, C. L. (1989). Peer acceptance of learning disabled children in the regular classroom. *Exceptional Children, 56*(1), 50-59.

Freeman, R. D., Goetz, E., Richards, D. P., & Groenveld, M. (1991). Defiers of negative prediction: A 14-year follow-up study of legally blind children. *Journal of Visual Impairment and Blindness, 85*(9), 365-370.

Fuchs, D., Fuchs, L. S., & Fernstrom, P. (1992, April). *A conservative approach to special education reform: Mainstreaming through transenvironmental programming and curriculum-based measurement.* Paper presented at the annual meeting of the American Educational Research Association, San Francisco.

Fuchs, L. S., & Deno, S. L. (1991). Paradigmatic distinctions between instructionally relevant measurement models. *Exceptional Children, 57*(6), 488-500.

Fuchs, L. S., & Fuchs, D. (1986). Curriculum-based assessment of progress toward long- and short-term goals. *The Journal of Special Education, 20,* 69-82.

Gage, N. L., & Berliner, D. C. (1991). *Educational psychology.* Boston: Houghton Mifflin.

Gallagher, J. (1979). Rights of the next generation. *Exceptional Children, 46*(2), 98-105.

Gallagher, J. J. (1990). New patterns in special education. *Educational Researcher, 19*(5), 34-36.

Gaylord-Ross, R. (Ed.). (1990-1992). *Issues and research in special education.* (Vols. 1-2). New York: Teachers College Press.

Gee, K., Graham, N., Goetz, L., Oshima, & Yoshioka, K. (1991). Teaching students to request the continuation of routine activities by using time delay and decreasing physical assistance in the context of chain interruption. *Journal of the Association for Persons with Severe Handicaps, 16*(3), 154-167.

Gelzheiser, L. M., & Meyers, J. (1992, April). *Pull-in and pull-out programs: A comparative case study.* Paper presented at the annual meeting of the American Education Research Association, San Francisco.

Glass, G. V., McGraw, G., & Smith, M. (1981). *Meta-analysis in social research*. Beverly Hills, CA: Sage.

Graf, V. L. (1992). Minimizing the inappropriate referral and placement of ethnic minority students in special education. In T. Cline (Ed.), *The assessment of special educational needs: International perspectives* (pp. 186-198). London: Routledge.

Guba, E. G., & Lincoln, Y. S. (1989). *Fourth generation evaluation*. Newbury Park, CA: Sage.

Guskin, S. (1984). Problems and promises of meta-analysis in special education. *Journal of Special Education, 18*(1), 73-80.

Hagen, C., Malkmus, D., Durham, P., & Bowman, K. (1979). Levels of cognitive functioning. In *Rehabilitation of the head injured adult: Comprehensive physical management* (pp. 87-89). Downey, CA: Professional Staff Association of Rancho Los Amigos Hospital.

Hahn, H. (1989). The politics of special education. In D. K. Lipsky & A. Gartner (Eds.), *Beyond special education: Quality education for all*. Baltimore: Brookes.

Hales, R. M., & Carlson, L. B. (1992). *Issues and trends in special education*. Lexington: University of Kentucky, Federal Resource Center for Special Education.

Hallahan, D., & Kauffman, J. (1978). *Exceptional children: Introduction to special education*. Englewood Cliffs, NJ: Prentice Hall.

Harding, S. (Ed.). (1987). *Feminism and methodology*. Bloomington: Indiana University Press.

Haring, T. G., & Laitinen, R. (1992). Extending complex repertoires of critical skills. In R. Gaylord-Ross (Ed.), *Issues and research in special education* (Vol. 2, pp. 125-155). New York: Teachers College Press.

Harris, S. L., Handleman, J. S., Gordon, R., Kristoff, & Fuentes, F. (1991). Changes in cognitive and language functioning of preschool children with autism. *Journal of Autism and Developmental Disorders, 21*(3), 281-290.

Hart, V. (1990). Handicapped infants. In M. C. Wang, M. C. Reynolds, & H. J. Walberg (Eds.), *Special education: Research and practice* (pp. 171-196). Oxford, UK: Pergamon.

Hays, W. L. (1988). *Statistics (for psychologists)*. New York: Holt, Rinehart & Winston.

Hedrick, T. E., Bickman, L., & Rog, D. J. (1993). *Applied research design*. Newbury Park, CA: Sage.

Heiman, G. (1992). *Basic statistics for the behavioral sciences*. Boston: Houghton Mifflin.

Henry, G. T. (1990). *Practical sampling*. Newbury Park, CA: Sage.

Heward, W. L., & Eachus, H. T. (1979). Acquisition of adjectives and adverbs in sentences written by hearing impaired and aphasic children. *Journal of Applied Behavior Analysis, 12*(3), 391-400.

Heward, W., & Orlansky, M. (1988). *Exceptional children: An introductory survey to special education*. Columbus, OH: Charles E. Merrill.

Higgins, P. C. (1992). Working at mainstreaming. In P. M. Ferguson, D. L. Ferguson, & S. J. Taylor (Eds.), *Interpreting disability: A qualitative reader* (pp. 103-123). New York: Teachers College Press.

Hocutt, A. M., McKinney, J. D., & Montague, M. (1993). Issues in the education of students with attention deficit disorder: Introduction to the special issue. *Exceptional Children, 60*(2), 103-106.

Hogan, T. P. (1975). *Survey of school attitudes*. New York: Harcourt Brace Jovanovich.

Howe, K. R., & Miramontes, O. B. (1991). A framework for ethical deliberation in special education. *The Journal of Special Education, 25*(1), 7-25.

Karchmer, M. A., Milone, M. N., & Wolk, S. (1979). Educational significance of hearing loss at three levels of severity. *American Annals of the Deaf, 124*, 97-109.

Kavale, K. (1984). Potential advantages of meta-analysis techniques for researchers in special education. *Journal of Special Education, 18*(1), 61-72.

Keller, C. (1993, April). *Paula: A girl with Down syndrome integrated in a sixth-grade classroom.* Paper presented at the 1993 annual meeting of the American Educational Research Association, Atlanta, GA.

Keller, C., Karp, J., & Carlson, H. L. (1993, April). *The community and school contexts for the integrations of students with disabilities in general education.* Paper presented at the 1993 annual meeting of the American Educational Research Association, Atlanta, GA.

Keough, B. K. (1990). Learning disability. In M. C. Wang, M. C. Reynolds, & H. J. Walberg (Ed.), *Special education: Research and practice* (pp. 119-142). Oxford, UK: Pergamon.

Kerlinger, F. N. (1973). *Foundations of behavioral research.* New York: Holt, Rinehart & Winston.

Keyser, D. J., & Sweetland, R. C. (1991). *Test critiques* (Vol. 7). Austin, TX: PRO ED.

Klin, A. (1991). Young autistic children's listening preferences in regard to speech: A possible characterization of the symptom of social withdrawal. *Journal of Autism and Developmental Disorders, 21*(1), 29-42.

Kluwin, T. N., & Moores, D. F. (1985). The effects of integration on the mathematics achievement of hearing impaired adolescents. *Exceptional Children, 52*(2), 153-160.

Koppenhaver, D. A., & Yoder, D. A. (1992). Literacy issues in persons with impairments. In R. Gaylord-Ross (Ed.), *Issues and research in special education* (Vol. 2). New York: Teachers College Press.

Krathwohl, D. R. (1993). *Methods of educational and social science research.* White Plains, NY: Longman.

Laing, J., & Farmer, M. (1984). *Use of the ACT assessment by examinees with disabilities.* (Research Report No. 84). Iowa City, IA: American College Testing Program.

Langenbach, M., Vaughn, C., & Aagaard, L. (1994). *An introduction to educational research.* Needham Heights, MA: Allyn & Bacon.

Lather, P. (1992). Critical frames in educational research: Feminist and poststructural perspectives. *Theory into Practice, 31*(2), 1-12.

Levitan, S. A. (1992). *Evaluation of federal social programs: An uncertain impact.* Washington, DC: George Washington University Center for Social Policy Studies.

Lincoln, Y. S., & Guba, E. G. (1985). *Naturalistic inquiry.* Beverly Hills, CA: Sage.

Lipsey, M. W. (1990). *Design sensitivity.* Newbury Park, CA: Sage.

Lipsky, D., & Gartner, A. (Eds.). (1989). *Beyond separate education: Quality for all.* Baltimore: Brookes.

MacMillan, D. L., Widaman, K. F., Balow, I. H., Hemsley, R. E., & Little, T. D. (1992). Difference in adolescent school attitudes as a function of academic level, ethnicity, and gender. *Learning Disabilities Quarterly, 15*(1), 39-50.

Marcaccio, K. Y. (1992). *Directory of online databases.* Detroit: Gale Research.

Marder, C., & Cox, R. (1990). More than a label: Characteristics of youth with disabilities. In M. Wagner, L. Newman, & D. L. Shaver (Eds.), *Young people with disabilities: How are they doing? A comprehensive report from wave 1 of the national longitudinal transition study of special education.* Menlo Park, CA: SRI International.

Marshall, C., & Rossman, G. B. (1989). *Designing qualitative research.* Newbury Park, CA: Sage.

Maruyama, G., & Deno, S. (1992). *Research in educational settings.* Newbury Park, CA: Sage.

Mastropieri, M. A., Scruggs, T. E., & Shiah, S. (1991). Mathematics instruction for learning disabled students: A review of research. *Learning Disabilities Research and Practice, 6*(2), 89-98.

McBurnett, K., Lahey, B. B., & Pfiffner, L. J. (1993). Diagnosis of attention deficit disorders in DSM-IV: Scientific basis and implications for education. *Exceptional Children, 60*(2), 108-117.

McGrew, K. S., Thurlow, M. L., & Spiegel, A. N. (1993). An investigation of the exclusion of students with disabilities in national data collection programs. *Educational Evaluation and Policy Analysis, 15*(3), 339-352.

McIntosh, R., Vaughn, S., Hager, D., & Okhee, L. (1993). Observations of students with learning disabilities in general education classrooms. *Exceptional Children, 60*(3), 249-261.

Meadow, K. (1980). *Deafness and child development.* Berkeley: University of California Press.

Meadow, K. P. (1967). *The effects of early manual communication and family climate on the deaf child's development.* Doctoral dissertation, University of California Berkeley.

Mehrens, W. A., & Lehmann, I. J. (1984). *Standardized tests in education.* New York: Holt, Rinehart & Winston.

Mertens, D. M. (1989). Social experiences of hearing impaired high school youth. *American Annals of the Deaf, 134*(1), 15-19.

Mertens, D. M. (1990a). Practical evidence of the feasibility of the utilization-focused approach to evaluation. *Studies in Educational Evaluation, 16,* 181-194.

Mertens, D. M. (1990b). A conceptual model of school placement and outcomes for the hearing-impaired student. In D. Moores & K. Meadow (Eds.), *Research in educational and developmental aspects of deafness* (pp. 25-72). Washington, DC: Gallaudet University Press.

Mertens, D. M. (1991a). Instructional factors related to hearing impaired adolescents' interest in science. *Science Education, 75*(4), 429-441.

Mertens, D. M. (1991b). Implications from the cognitive paradigm for teacher effectiveness research in deaf education. In D. S. Martin (Ed.), *Advances in cognition, education, and deafness* (pp. 342-347). Washington, DC: Gallaudet University Press.

Mertens, D. M. (1992). *Evaluation of the planning process for the project for inclusion of students in neighborhood schools: The total evaluation report.* Baltimore: Maryland State Department of Education.

Mertens, D. M. (1993a, November). *Empowerment through participatory evaluation in an international context.* Paper presented at the 1993 annual meeting of the American Evaluation Association, Dallas.

Mertens, D. M. (1993b, November). *Diverse voices: Feminist perspectives in evaluation.* Paper presented at the 1993 annual meeting of the American Evaluation Association, Dallas.

Mertens, D. M., Harper, J., Haigh, J., & Hayden, D. (1992, March). *Reclassification of exceptional students in Maryland.* Invited presentation at the 1992 Sixth Annual Conference on the Management of Federal/State Data Systems, Washington, DC.

Mertens, D. M., & Rabiu, J. (1992). Combining cognitive learning theory and computer assisted instruction for the deaf learner. *American Annals for the Deaf, 137*(5), 389-403.

Miles, M. B., & Huberman, A. M. (1984). *Qualitative data analysis.* Beverly Hills, CA: Sage.

Miller, D. C. (1991). *Handbook of research design and social measurement.* Newbury Park, CA: Sage.

Minter, M. E., Hobson, R. P., & Pring, L. (1991). Recognition of vocally expressed emotion by congenitally blind children. *Journal of Visual Impairment and Blindness, 85*(10), 411-415.

Moores, D. F. (1987). *Educating the deaf.* Boston: Houghton Mifflin.

Morris, L. L., Fitz-Gibbon, C. T., & Lindheim, E. (1987). *How to measure performance and use tests.* Newbury Park: Sage.

Mounty, J. L., & Anderson, B. T. (1993). *Assessment.* Paper presented at the 1993 annual meeting of the American Educational Research Association, Atlanta, GA.

NASDE. (1988). *NAEP testing for state comparisons: Issues related to the inclusion of handicapped students.* Washington, DC: National Association of State Directors of Special Education.

National Association of State Boards of Education. (1992). *Winners all: A call for inclusive schools.* Alexandria, VA: Author.

National Center on Educational Outcomes. (1991). *Assessing educational outcomes: State activity and literature integration.* Minneapolis: University of Minnesota.

National Commission on Excellence in Education. (1983). *A nation at risk: The imperative for educational reform.* Washington, DC: U.S. Department of Education.

Nielsen, J. M. (Ed.). (1990). *Feminist research methods: Exemplary readings in the social sciences.* Boulder, CO: Westview.

Odom, S. L. (1988). Research in early childhood special education: Methodologies and paradigms. In S. L. Odom & M. B. Karnes (Eds.), *Early intervention for infants and children with handicaps* (pp. 1-22). Baltimore: Brookes.

O'Donnell, L. M., & Livingston, R. I. (1991). Active exploration of the environment by young children with low vision: A review of the literature. *Journal of Visual Impairment and Blindness, 85*(7), 287-291.

Patton, M. Q. (1990). *Qualitative evaluation and research methods.* Newbury Park, CA: Sage.

Paul, P. V., & Quigley, S. P. (1990). *Education and deafness.* New York: Longman.

Peck, C. A., & Furman, G. C. (1992). Qualitative research in special education: An evaluative review. In R. Gaylord-Ross (Ed.), *Issues and research in special education* (Vol. 2, pp. 1-42). New York: Teachers College Press.

Pollard, G., & Oakland, T. (1985). Variables associated with the educational development of residential deaf children. *Special Services in the Schools, 1*(4), 67-82.

Popham, W. J., & Sirotnik, K. A. (1992). *Understanding statistics in education.* Itasca, IL: Peacock.

Reid, D., & Hresko, W. (1981). *A cognitive approach to learning disabilities.* New York: McGraw-Hill.

Reiff, H. B., Gerber, P. J., & Ginsberg, R. (1993). Definitions of learning disabilities from adults with learning disabilities: The insider's perspective. *Learning Disabilities Quarterly, 16*(3), 114-125.

Reinharz, S. (1992). *Feminist methods in social research.* New York: Oxford University Press.

Reschly, D. J. (1990). Mild mental retardation: Persistent themes, changing dynamics, and future prospects. In M. C. Wang, M. C. Reynolds, & H. J. Walberg (Eds.), *Special education: Research and practice* (pp. 81-100). Oxford, UK: Pergamon.

Reynolds, M. C., & Birch, J. W. (1977). *Teaching exceptional children in all America's schools.* Reston, VA: Council for Exceptional Children.

Roethlisberger, F. J., & Dickson, W. J. (1939). *Management and the worker*. Cambridge, MA: Harvard University Press.

Russell, N. K. (1993). Educational considerations in traumatic brain injury: The role of the speech-language pathologist. *Language, Speech, and Hearing Services in Schools, 24*, 67-75.

Schildroth, A. (1989). *Educational placement of hearing impaired students*. Paper presented at Gallaudet Research Institute Symposium, Washington, DC.

Schildroth, A. N., & Hotto, S. A. (1991). Annual survey of hearing impaired children and youth: 1989-90 school year. *American Annals of the Deaf, 136*(2), 155-164.

Scholl, G. T. (1990). Education of visually handicapped children and youth. In M. C. Wang, M. C. Reynolds, & H. J. Walberg (Eds.), *Special education: Research and practice* (pp. 161-170). Oxford, UK: Pergamon.

Schunk, D. H., & Rice, J. M. (1992). Influence of reading-comprehension strategy information on children's achievement outcomes. *Learning Disability Quarterly, 15*(1) 51-64.

Scruggs, T. E., & Mastropieri, M. A. (Eds.). (1992). *Advances in learning and behavior disabilities* (Vol. 7). Greenwich, CT: JAI Press.

Shapiro, E., & Lentz, F. E. (1991). Vocational-technical programs: Follow-up of students with learning disabilities. *Exceptional Children, 58*(1), 47-59.

Shaver, J. P. (1992, April). *What statistical significance testing is, and what it is not*. Paper presented at the annual meeting of the American Educational Research Association, San Francisco.

Shepard, L. A., Smith, M., & Vojir, C. (1983). Characteristics of pupils identified as learning disabled. *American Educational Research Journal, 20*, 309-331.

Sieber, J. E. (1992). *Planning ethically responsible research*. Newbury Park, CA: Sage.

Skrtic, T. M. (1991). *Behind special education*. Denver, CO: Love Publishing.

Slavin, R. E. (1987). Cooperative learning and the cooperative schools. *Educational Leadership, 45*(3), 7-13.

Smith, M. L. (1982). *How educators decide who is learning disabled*. Springfield, IL: Charles C Thomas.

Snyder, P., & Lawson, S. (1992, April). *Evaluating statistical significance using corrected and uncorrected magnitude of effect size estimates*. Paper presented at the annual meeting of the American Educational Research Association, San Francisco.

Spradley, J. P. (1980). *Participant observation*. New York: Holt, Rinehart & Winston.

Stainback, S., & Stainback, W. (1988). *Understanding and conducting qualitative research*. Dubuque, IA: Kendall/Hunt.

Stanfield, J. H. (1993). Methodological reflections. In J. H. Stanfield & R. M. Dennis (Eds.), *Race and ethnicity in research methods* (pp. 3-15). Newbury Park, CA: Sage.

Stanfield, J. H., & Dennis, R. M. (Eds.). (1993). *Race and ethnicity in research methods*. Newbury Park, CA: Sage.

Starlin, C. M. (1992, November). *Is performance based assessment the answer for students with disabilities?* Paper presented at the 1992 annual meeting of the American Evaluation Association, Seattle.

Stinson, D. M., Gast, D. L., Wolery, M., & Collins, B. C. (1991). Acquisition of nontargeted information during small-group instruction. *Exceptionality, 2*(2), 65-80.

Storey, K., & Horner, R. H. (1991). An evaluative review of social validation research involving persons with handicaps. *The Journal of Special Education, 25*(3), 352-401.

Sudman, S. (1976). *Applied sampling*. New York: Academic Press.

Suran, B. G., & Rizzo, J. V. (1983). *Special children: An integrative approach*. Glenview, IL: Scott, Foresman.

Switzky, H. N., & Heal, W. L. (1990). Research in speech education methods. In R. Gaylord-Ross (Ed.), *Issues and research in special education* (Vol. 1, pp. 1-81). New York: Teachers College Press.

Tawney, J. W., & Gast, D. L. (1984). *Single subject research in special education.* Columbus, OH: Charles E. Merrill.

Tesch, R. (1989). The computer-assisted analysis of qualitative data. In D. M. Mertens (Ed.), *Creative ideas for teaching evaluation* (pp. 165-174). Boston: Kluwer.

Tesch, R. (1990). *Qualitative research: Analysis types & software tools.* New York: Falmer.

Thesaurus of ERIC descriptors (12th ed.). (1990). Phoenix, AZ: Oryx Press.

Thesaurus of psychological index terms. (1988). Washington, DC: American Psychological Association.

Thompson, B. (1988, November). *Common methodology mistakes in dissertations: Improving dissertation quality.* Paper presented at the annual meeting of the Mid-South Educational Research Association, Louisville, KY. (ERIC Document Reproduction Service No. ED 301 595)

Thompson, B. (1992, April). *The use of statistical significance tests in research: Source criticisms and alternatives.* Paper presented at the annual meeting of the American Educational Research Association, San Francisco.

Thorndike, R. L., & Hagen, E. (1989). *Measurement and evaluation in psychology and education* (3rd ed.). New York: John Wiley.

Thurlow, M. L., Ysseldyke, J. E., & Silverstein, B. (1993). *Testing accommodations for students with disabilities.* Minneapolis: University of Minnesota, National Center on Educational Outcomes.

Tillman, M. H. (1973). Intelligence scales for the blind: A review with implications for research. *Journal of School Psychology, 11*(1), 80-87.

Towne, R. L., & Entwisle, L. M. (1993). Metaphoric comprehension in adolescents with traumatic brain injury and in adolescents with language learning disability. *Language, Speech, and Hearing Services in School, 24*, 100-107.

Trybus, R. J., & Karchmer, M. A. (1977). School achievement scores of hearing impaired children: National data on achievement status and growth patterns. *American Annals of the Deaf, 122*(4), 62-69.

U.S. Department of Education. (1989). *"To assure the free appropriate public education for all handicapped children": Eleventh annual report to Congress on the implementation of the Education of the Handicapped Act.* Washington, DC: Government Printing Office.

U.S. Department of Education. (1991). *"To assure the free appropriate public education of all children with disabilities": Thirteenth annual report to Congress on the implementation of the Individuals with Disabilities Education Act.* Washington, DC: Government Printing Office.

U.S. Department of Education. (1993a). *OSEP data dictionary.* Washington, DC: Office of Special Education Programs.

U.S. Department of Education. (1993b). *"To assure the free appropriate public education of all children with disabilities": Fifteenth annual report to Congress on the implementation of the Individuals with Disabilities Education Act.* Washington, DC: Government Printing Office.

U.S. Department of Education. (1993c). *Consumer guide.* Washington, DC: Office of Educational Research and Improvement.

U.S. Department of Health, Education, and Welfare. (1977). Assistance to states for education of handicapped children: Procedures for evaluating specific learning disabilities. *Federal Register, 42,* 65082-65085.

Van Cleve, J. V., & Crouch, B. A. (1989). *A place of their own.* Washington, DC: Gallaudet University Press.

Van Maanen, J. (1988). *Tales of the field: On writing ethnography.* Chicago: University of Chicago Press.

Wagner, M. (1992, April). *Being female—A secondary disability? Gender differences in the transition experiences of young people with disabilities.* Paper presented at the annual meeting of the American Educational Research Association, San Francisco.

Walker, D. K., Singer, J. D., Palfrey, J. S., Orza, M., Wenger, M., & Butler, J. A. (1988). Who leaves and who stays in special education: A 2 year follow up study. *Exceptional Children, 54*(5), 393-402.

Wang, M. C., Reynolds, M. C., & Walberg, H. J. (Eds.). (1987-1989). *Handbook of special education: Research and practice* (Vols. 1-3). Oxford, UK: Pergamon.

Wang, M. C., Reynolds, M. C., & Walberg, H. J. (Eds.). (1990). *Special education research and practice.* Oxford, UK: Pergamon.

White, K. R., Taylor, M. J., & Moss, V. D. (1992). Does research support claims about the benefits of involving parents in early intervention programs? *Review of Educational Research, 62*(1), 91-125.

Williams, C., Kantor, R., & Pinnell, G. S. (1992, April). *The language and literacy worlds of profoundly deaf preschool children: Informing developmental theory.* Paper presented at the 1992 annual meeting of the American Educational Research Association, San Francisco.

Willingham, W. W., Ragosta, M., Bennett, R. E., Braun, H., Rock, D. A., & Powers, D. A. (Eds.). (1988). *Testing handicapped people.* Boston: Allyn & Bacon.

Wilson, C. L., & Sindelar, P. T. (1991). Direct interaction in math word problems: Students with disabilities. *Exceptional Children, 57*(6), 512-519.

Winterling, V. (1990). The effects of constant time delay, practice in writing or spelling, and reinforcement on sight word recognition in a small group. *The Journal of Special Education, 24*(1), 101-116.

Wolff, A., & Harkins, J. (1986). Multihandicapped students. In A. Schildroth & M. Karchmer (Eds.), *Deaf children in America* (pp. 55-81). San Diego, CA: College-Hill.

Wood, F. H. (1990). Issues in the education of behaviorally disordered students. In M. C. Wang, M. C. Reynolds, & H. J. Walberg (Eds.), *Special education: Research and practice* (pp. 101-118). Oxford, UK: Pergamon.

Yin, R. K. (1989). *Case study research.* Newbury Park, CA: Sage.

Yin, R. K. (1993). *Applications of case study research.* Newbury Park, CA: Sage.

Ysseldyke, J. E., & Algozzine, B. (1990). *Introduction to special education* (2nd ed.). Boston: Houghton Mifflin.

Ysseldyke, J. E., Algozzine, B., & Epps, S. (1983). A logical and empirical analysis of current practice in classifying students as handicapped. *Exceptional Children, 50*(2), 160-166.

Ysseldyke, J. E., Algozzine, B., Shinn, M., & McGue, M. (1982). Similarities and differences among underachievers and students labeled learning disabled. *Journal of Special Education, 16,* 73-85.

Ysseldyke, J. E., Algozzine, B., & Thurlow, M. L. (1992). *Critical issues in special education.* Boston: Houghton Mifflin.

Ysseldyke, J. E., Thurlow, M. L., Bruininks, R. H., Gilman, C. J., Deno, S. L., McGrew, K. S., & Shriner, J. G. (1993). *Educational outcomes and indicators for individuals at the post-school level.* Minneapolis, MN: National Center on Educational Outcomes.

About the Authors

Donna M. Mertens is a Professor in the Department of Educational Foundations and Research at Gallaudet University. She teaches research methods, program evaluation, statistics, and educational psychology to deaf and hearing students at the B.A., M.A., and Ph.D. levels. She has conducted research and evaluation studies on such topics as improvement of special education services in international settings, enhancing the educational experiences of students with disabilities, reclassification of students with disabilities, planning for the inclusion of students with disabilities in neighborhood schools, and alternative service delivery models for special education. Her research has focused on the improvement of methods of inquiry by integrating the perspectives of those who have been oppressed in our society. Based on the writings of feminists and minorities who have addressed the issue of oppression and its implications for research methodology, she draws parallels to conducting research with persons with disabilities. She has made numerous presentations at the meetings of the American Educational Research Association, the American Evaluation Association, the Convention of American Instructors of the Deaf, and various international organizations that explore these themes. Her publications include an edited volume, titled *Creative Ideas for Teaching Evaluation*, as well as articles in *New Directions for Program Evaluation, Evaluation Practice, American Annals of the Deaf, Studies in Educational Evaluation*, and *Educational Evaluation and Policy Analysis*.

John A. McLaughlin is the Director of Research and Evaluation for the Virginia Department of Education. With his colleagues in the department, he has directed numerous studies focusing on such topics as the effects of varying class size and class mix on the performance of students with disabilities, and the impact of state policies on local educational practice. Prior to joining the department 3 years ago, he was Associate Professor of Curriculum and Instruction at Virginia Polytechnic Institute and State University, from 1978 to 1992, after being on the faculty of Utah State University and the University of Texas at Austin. During this time his research addressed various topics related to the education of students with disabilities, in particular, interagency collaboration as a vehicle to enhance service delivery to this population. His current interests center on the design, development, and use of performance measurement systems for public programs. He has served as the Annual Conference Chair for the American Evaluation Association for the past 3 years and is a consulting editor for the *Journal of Remedial and Special Education.*

Printed in the United States
4982

9 780803 948099